Oriental

APPETIZERS & LIGHT MEALS

Susan Fuller Slack

HPBooks

ACKNOWLEDGEMENTS

Bouquets of thank yous to Patricia J. Aaron, editor of *Oriental Appetizers & Light Meals,* to Editorial Director, Elaine R. Woodard, and the staff at HPBooks for their professionalism, skill and enthusiasm in creating this cookbook.

A very special thank you to my husband Bud and to my son Todd for their patience and support while I researched and wrote my book. And thanks to their determination and good cheer, which carried them in good stead, through countless meal-time hours of tasting, nibbling and snacking their way through this book from cover to cover.

Thanks to my sister Dee Bradney of Panama City, Florida for her energetic behind-the-scenes assistance in helping create the recipes and photographs, and to my good friends Shirley and Harlan Moore of Irvine, California for always being there to provide me with encouragement and a warm bed. Thanks to Jan and Richard Kilpatrick for their friendship and support, and for the endless hours logged at the computer on my behalf.

Thanks to my many friends throughout Southeast Asia for their invaluable help in researching this book by generously sharing their time and culinary talents. And to Lily Hataye of Santa Ana, California, for her educated palate and expertise in recipe testing.

ANOTHER BEST SELLING VOLUME FROM HPBOOKS
Photography & Food Styling: Burke/Triolo
Assistant Food Stylist: Susan Fuller Slack
Photo page 19, deGennaro Associates

HPBooks

A division of Price Stern Sloan, Inc.
360 North La Cienega Boulevard
Los Angeles, California 90048

©1987 HPBooks
Printed in U.S.A.
1st Printing

Cover Photo: Clockwise from top right: Shrimp & Kiwifruit in Lemon-Kimizu Dressing, page 66; Chinese Firecrackers, page 70, with Apricot Sauce, Curried Lamb Crescents with Pine Nuts & Apricot Sauce, page 44, Julienne Pear Salad with Lemon-Sesame Dressing, page 63; Skewered Pork, Vietnamese Pork Barbecue Platter, page 109.

Some accessories for photography were from New Stone Age, Los Angeles, CA and Freehand, Los Angeles, CA. Special thanks to Polly Murray, manager Consumer Services, McCormick & Company, Inc.

CONTENTS

SUSAN FULLER SLACK

Susan Fuller Slack is a native of Tennessee. It is often said that Tennesseans appreciate and value good friends and good food. They believe that without good friends, life is empty and without good food, one is empty. This tradition is an important part of Susan's life. As a successful food professional and busy wife who enjoys entertaining frequently, Susan has excelled in the art of cultivating both! She has developed a personal style of year-round entertaining which draws heavily upon influences from the Orient.

Her interest in the Asian cuisine began twelve years ago when she lived in Japan with her son Todd and husband Marine Corps Lieutenant Colonel Bud Slack. Although a world apart from the Smokey Mountains of Tennessee, Susan immediately felt that she had "come home." Japan and Tennessee happen to share the same latitude, with corresponding climates and seasons. The people of both regions share strong agricultural traditions, create unique handicrafts and prepare delicious foods utilizing available natural resources. Both share a deep love of nature. In March when the cherry blossoms bloom in Japan, the dogwoods bloom shortly thereafter in Tennessee!

Raised on Southern hospitality and heirloom cooking,

Susan quickly found that similar gestures of hospitality and good will were extended to guests in the Orient. In Hong Kong, China, Taiwan, Korea, the Philippines and other Southeast Asian countries, Susan was able to study the cuisines with famous chefs and teachers, in private homes and in restaurant kitchens.

From Newport, California to Newport, Rhode Island, Susan has instructed countless students on the theories and techniques of good cooking. She is well known in food circles for her expertise in Asian and French cooking, the pastry art, food processor techniques, food sculpting and children's cooking and is a certified member of the International Association of Cooking Professionals. She is the author of HPBooks' *Japanese Cooking*.

Currently living with her family in Annandale, Virginia, she writes food articles for newspapers and magazines and lectures on food and entertaining. Susan is a food stylist and consultant and enjoys creating special parties for discriminating palates throughout the Washington, D.C. area. She currently serves the Marine Officers' Wives Club of Washington, D.C. as Vice President. In her spare time, she enjoys traveling with her family to their Smokey Mountain vacation home in East Tennessee.

INTRODUCTION

The cuisines of Asia have been strongly influenced by two powerful big brothers, China and India. The overall pattern of Asia's civilization has developed in the shadow of these two great empires, not only in the area of cuisine, but in matters of government, religion, philosophy, culture and in the development of the people themselves. Centuries of trade and cultural exchange have created many similarities among the different types of cuisine in Asia, yet have in no way diminished the distinctive characteristics and nationalistic pride in each country's style of cooking. Geographical boundaries, western influences and availability of local foodstuffs have played an important role in helping each country retain its individuality.

However wide the spectrum of Asian cooking styles, every Asian cook strives to achieve the same goal in the kitchen: to prepare a variety of top-quality ingredients in contrasting, healthful ways which will enhance their natural flavors and textures. Chinese-influenced cooks are concerned with combining ingredients in ways which will yield a harmonious blending of the "five flavors" which are salty, bitter, spicy-hot, sweet and sour. A hallmark of all Asian cuisine is a carefully created balance in the tastes, colors, textures, aromas and appearance of foods.

In East Asia, proper food preparation is an art practiced and appreciated by people on all levels of society. The practice of using Chinese cooking techniques and foodstuffs has been assimilated into the cuisines of Korea, Japan and Formosa for thousands of years. Stir-frying was developed centuries ago in China when food and fuel were in short supply. The tenets of stir-frying are careful preparation, proper seasoning and quick cooking. These principles can be sucessfully used in the preparation of many of your favorite western foods. The Chinese discovered that cooking foods by steaming was fast and created a whole new dimension of textures and flavors. Steaming keeps foods moist, preventing them from drying out and burning. Chinese cuisine is memorable for its ingenious style of blending flavors. Several essential seasonings used in Chinese kitchens are soy sauce, vinegar, sugar, sesame seed oil, gingerroot, garlic, five-spice powder, Szechuan peppercorns, cilantro and star anise.

China can be divided geographically in four broad culinary regions. Cooking techniques and ingredients vary tremendously from provience to provience. Cooking styles from a variety of ethnic societies exist within the classification of the regional cuisines. The cooking of the southern provience of Kwantung is the most widely known in the West due to an influx of 19th century Chinese immigrants. Lightly seasoned Cantonese stir-fried dishes, steamed seafood dishes and a variety of delicious teahouse snacks characterize the cooking of the South.

In the heart of China lies Hupeh and Hunan, to the west lies Szechuan and Yunnan. These proviences are known for their spicy-hot and peppery foods. Other well-known foods are smoked meats and poultry, succulent, tender hams, hot and sour soups and dishes featuring the use of nuts and even dairy products. The cuisine of these regions has influenced the neighboring cuisines of Thailand, Viet Nam and Burma.

In the northern provinces, the cooking of the court aristocracy provided an elegant, refined touch to many dishes. Some of China's finest sweet and sour dishes come from this area. Wheat flour is one of the staple crops of the North, eaten profusely in the form of dumplings, noodles and bread. From Mongolia and Manchuria came the Muslim meat-eating tradition which popularized grilled mutton and lamb dishes. Hot-pot cooking and other dishes requiring slow cooking are especially popular in the cold northern regions. As in the south of China, the eastern coastal region is famous for its use of fresh-water and salt-water fish and shellfish. The eastern countryside is a rich agricultural area. In Shanghai, cold winters promote consumption of hearty foods such as noodle dishes and breads.

By virtue of its simplicity, the cuisine of Japan stands apart from Chinese cuisine. For centuries, Buddhism forbade eating meat. Japanese cooks have had to make good use of the generous bounty from the sea and of yields from the limited amount of cultivable land. Japanese taste is based upon a complex blending of amino acids found in natural seasonings and simple foods such as dried sea vegetation, dried seafood, dried mushrooms, soy sauce, fermented bean paste (miso), rice vinegar and rice wine. Tea, tofu and soy sauce were introduced from China.

Korean cuisine has often been regarded as a casual blending of the neighboring cuisines of China and Japan. Despite these strong influences, the spirited Koreans have preserved their unique culinary ways. Korean food is highly seasoned, robust and liberally laced with red peppers, garlic and green onions. Sesame seeds, sesame seed oil, soy sauce, rice vinegar and gingerroot are everyday seasonings. Beef is the favorite meat, often marinated and grilled over charcoal or simmered to make one-pot dishes or hearty soups. Chicken, seafood, sea vegetables and a vast array of cultivated and wild land vegetables are eaten regularly.

In the subcontinent of India and Pakistan, the cuisine is noted for its skillful blending of spices and herbs. This method of seasoning and preserving foods has spread widely through most of the countries of Southeast Asia. The reign of the mightly Moghul empire brought about a period of magnificence and opulence in the cuisine of Pakistan and India which has never been paralleled. Strong Persian influences added a touch of elegance and refinement. Delicious rice pilafs, braised and tandoori roasted lamb, koftas, kabobs and the use of saffron, dairy products and edible gold leaf to decorate foods are Moghul touches.

In the southern coastal areas of India, seafood dishes are unequalled in variety and quality. Steaming, deep-frying and sautéing are common cooking methods. Three major religions have played an important role in the development of Indian and Pakistani cuisine. The Muslims eat no pork and often no seafood, preferring beef and lamb. The majority of Indians are Hindus who refrain from eating beef or dairy products. Indian Buddhists are staunch vegetarians. Indians traditionally eat their foods by scooping up small portions with their right hands. The left hand is considered unclean for eating. Spoons and forks are commonly used in India today.

Southeast Asia includes the countries of Thailand, Burma, Viet Nam, the Philippine Islands, Malaysia, Singapore and Indonesia. Thailand is a food lover's paradise offering a wealth of natural resources. Thai food has a unique taste, redolent of hot chilies, aromatic spices, garlic, gingerroot, lemongrass, tangy tamarind, fresh cilantro and salty fish sauce. The Thais make delicious custards and sweet snacks from coconut milk, sweet glutinous rice and fresh tropical fruits. Foods in Thailand are traditionally eaten with a spoon or a fork.

In Viet Nam, foods are characterized by the use of salty fish sauce, fresh mint and other herbs, aromatic spices, peanuts, rice noodles, seafood, fresh fruits and vegetables. Foods are often served with lettuce leaves for wrapping before they are eaten. The popularity and availability of authentic French-style breads is a direct legacy from France. Foods are eaten with chopsticks, the same as in China.

In the Philippine Islands, strong Chinese, Malay, Polynesian, Spanish and American influences have helped to shape the cuisine. Often westernized, Filipino foods are cooked in a simple style, often by braising, sautéing and deep-frying. Filipinos always observe the Spanish custom of serving a daily snack with afternoon tea, a tradition called a "merienda." A simple western-style cake or cookies or a native sweet made with coconut milk and rice might be served. "Merienda sienna" is similar to a high tea and constitutes the serving of a full meal. No rice is served.

Malaysian food is an intriguing blend of the multiracial cuisines of native Malayia and Chinese and Indian immigrants. Eurasians and British colonialists have added their influence, although to a lesser degree. In spite of such diversity, the cuisine of each Malaysian state has retained its own style of cooking, each with a distinctive taste.

The foods of Singapore represent all of these groups and many more. Singapore and Malaysia are especially famous for their Nonya or Straits Chinese cuisine. Nonyas are women descendents of Chinese immigrant laborers who married native Malay men. Their cuisine is a blend of Chinese and Malay cuisines. Because of shared cultures, the foods of Malaysia and Singapore are similar to the East Indies. This tropical island chain has been the recipient of thousands of years of cultural and culinary exchange with India, Polynesia, China, Portugal, the Middle East and with the Dutch who colonized Indonesia in the early 1600's. Like Malaysian food, Indonesian food is very spicy from the copious use of hot chili peppers.

Within all these countries, everyday family meals and communal dining and feasting promote a delightful ambience, which is a regular way of life.

ORIENTAL ENTERTAINING

Emerging cooking trends from the East have greatly influenced America's tastes and her tables. We have experienced a blending of oriental "know-how" with quality indigenous American products resulting in the development of a new emerging American cuisine. The origin of France's nouvelle cuisine actually began in the Orient. The emphasis on preparing foods quickly and simply while enhancing their fresh, natural flavors, interesting textures and beautiful colors, is a direct reflection of the oriental philosophy of food preparation. By embracing the best of this creative and healthful new approach to food preparation, we will delight our family and friends with delicious and imaginative Asian-style meals.

You can build your party menus, creating splendid partnerships of compatible dishes from countries throughout the Orient. Be guided by the same principals you use in planning occidental-style meals. Select dishes which meet your nutritional needs and offer a variety of interesting contrasts in texture, temperature, flavor and color. Do not select too many dishes which are highly seasoned; usually one or two is enough. Simple menus are suitable for a family-style meal in which all of the dishes are placed on

the table at one time. Increase the number of dishes accordingly for banquet-style meals which are traditionally served in courses. Select do-ahead dishes, including only one dish which requires last-minute cooking. Except for noodle dishes, snack foods and sweets, always accompany your foods with plenty of plain or embellished cooked rice which is almost always regarded in Asia as the most important food eaten during any meal.

Perhaps like me, you can appreciate and be inspired by the enthusiasm of gentleman scholar Li Li Weng who believed that "Guests should be served something special. I often suggest to the little woman that she gather the dew which collects on flowers. When the rice is just cooked, pour a little of the dew on it, and let it stand, covered, for a little while. The guests thought that I had served some special grain, but it was only ordinary rice." While your pursuit in serving delicious Asian cuisine need not go to such an extreme, you can always foster a sense of adventure and create an element of surprise by adding that special touch! Harmony will reign in your kitchen, surely a sign that the ancient Chinese negative and positive forces of yin and yang are peacefully in balance.

ENTERTAINING WITH FLAIR

Entertaining allows us the opportunity to share good food and good conversation with friends, providing an outlet to relieve the tensions of the day and add to our mental and social well-being. This act of sharing with friends is in itself a celebration of life. When we entertain, we should strive to express our own personalities. Planning a party is much like creating an original painting. We begin both with an empty canvas and with an assortment of colors from which to choose.

Although each of us will begin our "painting" with the same colors, they will never turn out exactly the same. With every brush stroke, the finished product becomes an expression of our personality. And so it is with entertaining. We are allowed to be innovative and sharing of ourselves and the things that we love. A mood of enchantment is spread which enables our family and friends to experience and savor the unique flavor which we create as individuals.

The intriguing, sometimes exotic styles of cuisine found throughout the Far East can add a new dimension to your personal style of home entertaining and enable you to create unique and individualized parties. From the simplicity and subtleness of Japanese sushi to the assertive, spicy-hot curries found in Indonesia, you will discover a medley of flavors, textures, colors and cooking styles in this cookbook. Browse through the chapters to select recipes and menus which will please even the most discriminating palate. The recipes stress naturalness and emphasize the use of fresh seasonal foods, seasoned effectively to gratify the palate, and prepared in a healthful, straightforward manner.

Becoming organized is the key to successful entertaining. Plan carefully and shop well in advance, leaving little to chance. Make lists to keep the details straight. Don't overlook the smaller details: cocktail napkins, chopstick rests, ice cubes, candles or steaming perfumed hot towels for guests to wipe their hands on after their meal.

To become completely familiar with the recipes and menus, try them out on your family first. If you are a novice oriental cook, begin by incorporating one or two of the Asian recipes into a suitable western-style menu you enjoy preparing for parties. Try cooking and refrigerating or freezing some foods ahead such as the stuffed steamed buns, dumplings, curries or chutneys. Preparing ahead is especially important when dealing with large amounts of food for larger parties. Shop and cook in stages, not in one exhausting spree. Because it is important to be a guest at your own party, most of the recipes in this book can be prepared completely in advance. The ingredients for dishes which can't be cooked ahead, such as the stir-fry dishes, can be assembled in advance requiring only quick last-minute cooking. Finish all the last-minute preparations early enough to allow time for you to relax and feel calm when your guests arrive.

It is fun to create authentic table settings and centerpieces for your parties and special meals. It isn't a prerequisite to go out and immediately buy a complete stock of Asian-style props or a matched set of oriental dishes. It's fun and often easy to improvise. In Asia, dishes are often designed to match the foods, not necessarily each other. Your table setting can be a mismatched collection of favorite small bowls, dishes and baskets. Small unusual ceramic ashtrays are often attractive enough to be used as dishes. Bamboo or woven cloth placemats are attractive and will protect a dining table with a wooden top. If the cost of fresh flowers is prohibitive, arrange two or three stunning flowers, Japanese-style, in an oriental-style container. Create an exquisite centerpiece featuring one large beautiful flower carved from an onion or a round root vegetable. Set aside a closet or even one or two shelves to assemble your collection of special dishes and containers which you can use over and over again in creative, imaginative ways.

When serving your carefully prepared foods, never bring them to the table "unadorned." Select appropriate platters or containers on which to display your food. Old, sometimes forgotten serving pieces can be used in new and unusual ways. The addition of a simple, edible garnish can turn your foods into a beautiful sight. Although the foods should be attractive enough to speak for themselves, edible decorations and garnishes are meant to enhance foods, not hide them. Properly executed, simplicity becomes elegance.

Thousand Flowers Appetizer Basket, pages 10-11

Thousand Flowers Appetizer Basket *China*

Food sculpting is an ancient art form long practiced in the oriental culture. The devotion of the Asian people to beautiful flowers is evident in every aspect of their lives. Recreate this edible Asian-influenced flower basket and "let one-thousand flowers bloom." The basket can be filled one day ahead, enclosed in a plastic bag and refrigerated overnight. Spray parsley occasionally with cool water. Your table will blossom with color, lending an exotic air of enchantment to the occasion. Invite guests to "pluck" the flowers for nibbling, if they wish. Serve your favorite dip on the side. Hua Hsien, the Chinese Goddess of flowers, and the handmaidens who carry her flower baskets, would certainly approve! (Photo on page 9.)

Oasis to secure flower arrangement
1 medium-size basket or other imaginative container
Bunches of fresh Italian parsley or parsley
Fresh flowering herbs, if desired
Edible flowers, if desired
1 recipe Celestial Bread-Dough Butterflies, page 52, if desired
8- to 10-inch bamboo skewers

Frosted Mushrooms:
2 (3-oz.) packages cream cheese, room temperature
Prepared Japanese horseradish (wasabi) to taste
1 to 2 drops green food coloring, if desired
8 to 10 medium-size fresh mushrooms, tops wiped
Fresh shiso leaves or parsley, minced, or black Dry Roasted Sesame Seeds,
    page 24

Instant Flowers:
Whole fresh chives
Miniature cocktail ears of corn
Broccoli florets, blanched 30 seconds, chilled in iced water
Cauliflower florets
Lotus root slices, soaked in a vinegar-water bath
Asparagus stalks, blanched 30 seconds, chilled in iced water
Edible pea pods, blanched 30 seconds, chilled in iced water
Pickled ginger shoots
Japanese pickled plums (umeboshi)
Medium-size to large shrimp, cooked, peeled, deveined
Hard-cooked quail eggs, peeled

Cut Flowers:
Large and small carrots, scraped
Japanese white radishes (daikons)
Jicima, thinly sliced
Japanese or European-style cucumbers, thinly sliced
Medium-size well-shaped radishes, thinly sliced
Sliced raw beets, blanched, thinly sliced
Food coloring, if desired
Steamed Japanese fish loaf (kamaboko), thinly sliced

Fantasy Flowers:
Green onion stems
Root ends of green onions
Food coloring, if desired
Fresh whole red, green or yellow chili peppers
Cherry tomatoes
Small round red or white onions, skins removed
Whole Japanese pickles
Brussel sprouts, blanched 30 seconds, chilled in iced water
Cauliflower florets
Carrot slices

Place oasis in basket. If using Italian parsley, arrange loosely in oasis. If using parsley, remove rubber band from 1 bunch of parsley; shape in an evenly rounded bouquet. Remove loose stems; reposition at side of bunch. Replace rubber band. Repeat with remaining parsley. Pack basket with parsley so skewered vegetable-flowers will stand when inserted into place. Prepare Frosted Mushrooms, Instant Flowers, Cut Flowers and Fantasy Flowers, as desired.

Push Frosted Mushrooms, Instant Flowers, Cut Flowers and Fantasy Flowers deep into oasis; insert at random striving to create a casual full symmetrical bouquet. Add herbs and edible flowers, if desired. Freshness and naturalness are the only guidelines. Strive to link your arrangement to the corresponding season. If desired, insert bamboo skewers into several Celestial Bread-Dough Butterflies and tuck into basket; serve remaining butterflies in a basket.

Frosted Mushrooms:
In a small bowl, combine cream cheese, horseradish and food coloring, if desired. Frost tops of mushrooms with cheese mixture; sprinkle with shiso leaves. Insert bamboo skewers into mushrooms. Use leftover cheese for binding small flower parts.

Instant Flowers:
Select desired foods. Pat dry chilled vegetables. Insert bamboo skewers into flowers.

Cut Flowers:
Cut carrots in thin slices or scoop in small balls. Cut food slices in floral shapes using assorted sizes of metal cookie or canape cutters. Dye white flower shapes in small amounts of water tinted with food coloring, if desired. Trim fish loaf slices in interesting shapes or leave plain. Combine a variety of colors and shapes and assemble on bamboo skewers to form an assortment of flower shapes.

Fantasy Flowers:
Shred a 1-inch portion of trimmed green onion stem in a flower. Use longer green stems as stem-like covers for bamboo skewers. Use stringy root-ends of green onions as flowers; dye with food coloring, if desired. With kitchen scissors, cut chilies in eighths; do not cut completely through stem end. Rinse out seeds. Drop into a bowl of iced water; keep separate from other flowers. Warn guests of fiery character of innocent-looking flowers. Cut cherry tomatoes in quarters without completely cutting through to stem end. Remove seeds. Insert a V-shape wedge cutting tool or small paring knife midway into side of a small onion and make V-shape cuts completely around onion, cutting 1/2 of way into onion. Repeat with remaining onions. Hold onions under hot running water; separate layers. Tint with food coloring, if desired. Cut Japanese pickles in fan-shapes; spread gently to open. Assemble Fantasy Flowers on bamboo skewers. Carefully separate brussel sprouts leaves. Reassemble 4 to 6 of nicest leaves on a bamboo skewer in a circular pattern with cupped sides up. Attach a cauliflower floret or carrot slice center.

Charm your guests with delightful and unique fare at both casual and formal gatherings. Several of the following menus consist of "mix-and-match" recipes from countries throughout Asia. With careful thought and planning, other recipes in this cookbook can be combined in diverse ways to create a perfect balance within the structure of a composed menu. Consider the flavors, texture and colors of each dish in a menu; keep them varied, yet always complementary.

HOMESPUN HARVEST SUPPER

Turkey Kebabs in Creamed Spinach
(page 92)
*Perfumed Basmati Rice
Swirled with Saffron & Rose Water*
(page 91)
Oven-Baked Cranberry-Cardamon Chutney
(page 127)
Yam & Peanut Cracker-Bread
(page 86)
Pastry Pumpkins with Green Tea Ice Cream
(page 153)
Ceylon tea steeped with cardamon

PROGRESSIVE DINNER FOR THE GOURMET CLUB

First course
Indonesian Chicken Soup
(page 54)
Second course
*Cinnamon-Scented Roast Duck Salad
in Egg-Flour Wrappers*
(pages 64-65)
*Indonesian-Style Butterfly Leg of Lamb
with Satay Peanut Sauce*
(page 123)
Chinese-Style Steamed Sandwich Buns
(page 116)
Third Course
Indonesian-Style Pineapple Dessert Centerpiece
(page 156)
*Spiced Macadamia Nut Cake
with Coconut-Lime Glaze*
(page 146)
Coffee with cardamon, Hot Ginger Tea
(page 143)

JAPANESE "COOK-IT YOURSELF" PIZZA PARTY

Shrimp & Onion Fritters
(page 80)
Japanese-Style Pizza
(pages 104-105)
Vietnamese Pickled Julienne of Vegetables
(page 134)
Spiced Green Tea Ice Cream
(page 152)
Japanese green tea (sencha), soft drinks, cold beer

SUPER NOODLE BOWL SUNDAY

Filipino Stir-Fried Shrimp & Pancit Canton
(page 89)
Lu Chu Pot Roast Noodles
(page 102)
Hot & Sour Cucumber Sticks
(page 133)
Meiko's Ginger-Flavored Sweet Wine Cake
(page 147)
Soft drinks, cold beer

FOURTH OF JULY CELEBRATION

Chinese Firecrackers
(page 70)
Korean-Style Grilled Beef Short Ribs
(page 121)
*Crispy Potato Julienne
with Red Pepper & Green Onion Sauce*
(page 78)
Julienne Pear Salad with Lemon-Sesame Dressing
(page 63)
Coconut Ice Cream
(page 151)
Soft drinks, cold beer

EIGHT PRECIOUS FRIENDS
TEA-LUNCH

Mandarin Orange Fruit Soup
(page 53)
Chicken Packets with Eight Precious Condiments
(pages 62-63)
*Steamed Egg Buns Stuffed with
Honey Roast Pork & Oyster Sauce*
(page 106)
Teahouse Golden Custard Tartlets
(page 148)
*Chinese jasmine tea, Chinese lychee black tea or lo
cha friendship tea (oolong tea
with lychee flowers)*

BRIDAL LUNCHEON BUFFET

Thousand Flowers Appetizer Basket
(pages 10-11)
Assortment of favorite dips
Princess Hats
(pages 40-41)
Thousand Year Sauce Chicken
(page 98)
Spicy Pork with Bamboo Shoots in Pastry Baskets
(pages 84-85)
Caramelized Lemon Shrimp
(pages 88-89)
Taiwanese Pineapple Wedding Cake
(page 145)
*Chinese jasmine tea, English breakfast tea or
Chinese keemum black tea steeped with
dried rose petals*

TIFFIN FOR SIX

Lesley's Goan Coconut-Chicken Curry
(page 99)
*Perfumed Basmati Rice
Swirled with Saffron & Rosewater*
(page 91)
Curried Pear Chutney with Fresh Ginger
(page 128)
Rose Dumplings
(page 150)
Darjeeling tea steeped with cloves and cinnamon

AFTERNOON DELIGHT

Sweet & Spicy Dip for Fresh Fruit
(page 134)
Pink Rice-Stick Noodles with Seafood & Vegetables
(page 100)
*Sweetened iced tea steeped with fresh mint and
sliced fresh gingerroot*

HEARTS & CHOPSTICKS
VALENTINE'S DAY LUNCHEON

Creamy Asparagus Soup with Crabmeat
(page 51)
Glazed Walnut Sushi Roll
(pages 76-77)
Honey Roast Pork
(page 108)
*Luzon Shrimp & Hearts of Palm Salad
with Creamy Lime Vinaigrette*
(page 60)
Rose Ice Cream
(page 151)
The Ultimate Chinese Almond Cookie
(page 154)
Orange pekoe tea flavored with Rose Syrup
(page 150)

HOLIDAY MINI-BUFFET FOR
COCKTAILS

Shrimp & Pork Rissoles
(pages 34-35)
Sesame-Tofu Meatballs
(page 33)
Cranberry-Orange Dipping Sauce
(page 137)
Orange-Flavored Beef
(page 41)
Chinese-Style Steamed Sandwich Buns
(page 116)
*Peking-Style Smoked Turkey
with Cornmeal Pancakes*
(page 113)
Szechuan Marinated Vegetables
(page 132)
Autumn Moon Cakes
(pages 142-143)

GLOSSARY OF INGREDIENTS

Easy to obtain ingredients have been used in the recipes in this cookbook. You can shop and cook from foods available in supermarkets and oriental or gourmet food stores.

Cornstarch: Used in Southeast Asian cooking to produce satiny-smooth translucent sauces, in marinades to help keep meats moist and velvetize textures and to seal in natural juices when used for coating deep-fried foods. Has twice the thickening power of flour. Dissolve in cool liquid. Stir a cornstarch and liquid mixture before adding to hot foods; has a tendency to settle to bottom of bowl.

Hoisin Sauce: (soy jam) A thick, sweet, spicy commercial Chinese sauce containing fermented soy beans, vinegar, sugar, garlic, chili and spices. Use as "Chinese ketchup", a dipping sauce, a seasoning in stir-fried dishes or for making Asian-style barbecue sauce.

Konbu: (kelp) A brown algae of the genus Laminaria. A primary ingredient for making Japanese fish stock. Blades of kelp are harvested, sun-dried and folded in smooth sheets. Wipe very lightly. Place in bottom of pan when simmering vegetables and other foods to enhance flavors.

Mirin: Slightly syrupy rice wine made from sweet glutinous rice, a mold (koji) and a fiery distilled 90 proof liquor (shochu). Indispensible in Japanese cooking, adding sweetness to foods and an attractive glaze. Contributes to luster of sushi rice. Purchase high-quality mirin with no added preservatives.

Miso: Japanese fermented soybean paste. Resembles peanut butter in consistency, but comes in a variety of colors and textures, each with its own aroma and flavor. Three basic categories are rice miso, soybean miso and barley miso. Progenitor of a wide variety of fermented bean paste used in Southeast Asia today. Other familiar types are Chinese hoisin sauce, Szechuan hot soybean paste, oyster sauce, Korean red pepper paste (kochu jang), and Vietnamese fish sauce (nuoc mam).

Nori: (laver) A highly prized algae of the genus Porphyra Tenera. Select rich, black, unfolded sheets with a shiny surface. The better the color, the higher the quality. Use for making rolled sushi or snip in shreds to garnish rice, noodles, soups or salads. Toast before using.

Oyster Sauce: A rich-tasting, thick brown oyster-flavored sauce made from oyster extracts. Use sparingly to enhance flavor of sauces, soups and stir-fried dishes, or use as a dipping sauce for appetizers. Best-flavored, top-quality brands come from Hong Kong.

Pandanus Leaf: (screwpine leaf) A long, tapering green leaf used in Thailand, Viet Nam and the East Indies to flavor rice, syrups, pastries and sweets. Leaves are crushed to release warm, nutty flavor and fragrance before being added to foods. Flavor of pandanus leaves is as popular in Southeast Asia as vanilla is in the West. Its green extract can be found in Southeast Asian markets.

Panko: Pressed, dried bread crumbs used in Japanese cooking for coating deep-fried foods. Makes an excellent coating which stays crispy for hours.

Rice Flour: Flour made from finely ground rice. One type is made from finely ground cooked sweet glutinous rice. It is used for making sweet confections and rice cakes throughout Southeast Asia. Look for the Japanese rice flour called mochiko.

Rice Vinegar: Distilled from white rice. Has a natural sweetness and flavor milder than American white vinegar. Excellent for pickling and making salad dressings. Helps reduce discoloration of certain vegetables and soften fibers of vegetables during cooking.

Rose Water: Made from diluted rose essence extracted from fragrant deep-red rose petals. Used in India for making a variety of sweet and savory dishes as well as in beverages. Also used in Thai cooking and sometimes in special Chinese dishes. Purchase in drugstores, gourmet shops, Asian markets or Middle Eastern markets.

Sake: Japanese wine brewed from steamed rice, a special mold (koji) and high quality spring water. Alcohol content ranges from 12 to 15 percent. Amino acids in sake act as a tenderizer on meats and seafood. Dispells strong food odors and flavors. Acts as a balancing agent for other salty seasonings such as soy sauce.

Sesame Seed Oil: Aromatic, pressed, amber-colored oil of toasted sesame seeds. Rarely used as a cooking oil because high temperatures burn oil and destroy distinctive flavor. Add to marinades and sauces or add sparingly after stir-frying dishes for fragrance and flavor. An excellent table seasoning. Do not substitute cold-pressed oil found in health food stores which is processed from untoasted sesame seeds

Shiitake: Earthy-tasting, flavorful black forest mushrooms which grow on oak logs. Available fresh or dried. Purchase with thick dark caps with edges slightly curled under. Best quality has well-defined cracks running through tops. Dried mushrooms have a more intense, meaty flavor than fresh mushrooms. Rehydrate dried mushrooms in warm water. Soaking water can be used to flavor glazes, sauces and soups, or treat your houseplants to a healthy drink.

Shrimp Paste: Used throughout Southeast Asia, especially East India and Thailand. Made from tiny shrimp which are fermented or decomposed to a certain degree and preserved through heavy salting. Dried form is sold in dark brown cakes. Must be cooked before use. Fishy flavors and odors mellow after cooking and enhance flavors of cooked foods. Substitute anchovy paste or omit entirely.

Southeast Asian Fish Sauce: (Vietnam, "nuoc mam"; Thailand, "nampla"; Philippines, "patis"; Indonesia, "petis") Thin light-brown salty fermented fish sauce used extensively as a seasoning in many Southeast Asian countries much the same way soy sauce is used in China or Japan. Adds depth of flavor and enhances natural taste of foods without leaving an objectional fishy taste or smell. Composition of different sauces vary from country to country, but are basically interchangeable in use.

Soy Sauce: Introduced into Japan by Chinese Buddhist priests in sixth century. Japan developed a lighter, more refined product. Made from cultured soybeans and wheat; resulting mash is combined with brine and fermented. Aged mash is strained and pressed to obtain light soy sauce. Longer aged mash is pressed to obtain dark soy sauce. A major seasoning ingredient in Chinese, Japanese, Korean, Indonesian, Malaysian and Filipino cooking. Amino acids formed from soybean protein are components which heighten taste sensations and enhance natural flavors of foods. Used as a favorite seasoning around the world. Do not substitute domestic-made supermarket brands, except Kikkoman, for Chinese or Japanese brands. Others are chemically fermented from substances treated with hydrochloric acid. Buy in small amounts.

Tamarind: Bean-shaped pods with a tart-tasting dark-brown sticky fibrous fruit. Soak fruit pulp in hot water to obtain tamarind water which is used throughout Southeast Asia as a souring agent, or purchase tamarind concentrate and dilute with water. Substitute fresh lemon or lime juice.

Tofu: A white custard-like food substance made from soy milk. Three main types are available: firm Chinese-style, slightly less-firm regular Japanese-style and soft or silken Japanese-style. Look for well-chilled packages with fresh clear packing water and stamped with a pull-date for quality control. Rinse and submerge in a bowl of cool water. Refrigerate up to 7 days, changing water daily. Refresh older, slightly sour tofu by blanching 2 to 3 minutes in boiling water; use in dishes which require cooking.

Vegetable Oils: Use top-quality peanut or corn oil for deep-frying. Peanut oil can be heated to higher temperatures. Oil used for deep-frying can be reused one or two times if it still looks light and clear. Skim surface of oil during frying; strain after each use. Refresh used oil by frying several slices of peeled gingerroot until light-brown. A combination of used and new oil will produce a golden-colored finish on fried foods. Use corn or safflower oil for stir-frying.

Wine: Dry white wine is used in Chinese cooking to neutralize odors such as those found in seafood. Added to meat and seafood marinades, glazes and sauces. Chinese cooks use Shaoshing or Chinese rice wine. If not available, substitute good-quality pale dry sherry. Do not substitute Japanese sake or Japanese sweet rice wine, mirin. Never use wines labeled cooking wines. They are too salty and lack fragrance and taste.

Yogurt: A custard-like food made by adding a bacterial culture to whole milk and fermenting. As bacteria reproduce, the milk sugar (lactose) changes into lactic acid, causing milk to thicken or curdle and create a distinctive, tangy taste. In India and Pakistan, yogurt is made with buffalo's milk and eaten daily in many forms.

HERBS & SPICES

Herbs and spices define the cuisine of a country more than cooking techniques or food staples. They have helped to create the unique flavors of the variety of foods found throughout the countries of Southeast Asia. Imagine the taste of Italian pizza or spaghetti sauce without basil or oregano, American gingerbread without the flavor of ground ginger or Chinese food without the spiceness of fresh gingerroot. They certainly wouldn't taste the same!

HERBS

Herbs are aromatic leaves of plants grown primarily in temperate zones. Use fresh herbs whenever possible; refrigerate wrapped in damp paper towels and placed in zip-type plastic bags. Fresh herbs can be frozen for long periods if properly wrapped. Replace ground herbs every six months. Whole, dried herbs retain their flavoring oils longer. Store dried herbs in airtight containers in refrigerator or in a cool, dark place away from heat and light. Dried herbs are stronger tasting than fresh herbs. To substitue dried herbs, use one-third of the amount of fresh herbs.

Basil Leaves: Native to India, this ancient leafy green herb from the mint family is used in East Indian, Indian, Pakistani and Thai cooking. Use sweet basil or lemon basil. Much of dried basil sold in supermarkets comes from California.

Bay Leaf: Favored in Southeast Asian cooking, especially in India, East India and China, is the cassia tree leaf (Cinnamomum cassia). Bark of this tree is commonly sold as cinnamon. Subtle flavor of the Asian bay leaf is usually more suitable to Asian cooking. If unavailable, look for Turkish bay leaves. If using stronger flavored California bay laurel leaves, cut amount by half.

Cilantro Leaves: (Chinese parsley) Member of the carrot family (Umbelliferae). One of oldest known spices in the world, dating back to 5,000 B.C. Resembles flat-leaf parsley. Used extensively in Southeast Asian cooking for its distinctive flavor and as a garnish. Added to curries, stir-fry dishes, soups, sauces and chutneys. No real flavor substitute.

Lemongrass: (citronella) Tall green stalks of grass which add an aromatic lemon-citrus flavor. Tender inner stalks are smashed, sliced or minced and added to stir-fry and braised dishes, marinades, soups and sauces. Tough outer stalks can be pounded and added to simmered or steamed foods; discard stalks after foods are cooked. Substitute thin outer peel of fresh lemons.

Mint: Aromatic green leafy herb used regularly in Vietnamese, Thai, Indian and East Indian cooking. Fresh spearmint is excellent for Southeast Asian cooking. Easy to grow and a fast-spreading addition to a herb garden.

Shiso: (perilla) Bright-green leaf of the beefsteak plant has a pleasant, minty taste. Used in sushi and other Japanese dishes. Red variety used in Japanese pickling. Easy to grow, making it an excellent addition to a herb garden. No flavor substitute.

SPICES

Spices are aromatic dried berries, seeds and bark of plants and trees which grow in tropical areas. Buy small amounts of whole spices and grind as needed in an electric coffee mill or spice mill to preserve flavoring oils. Companies which sell herbs and spices usually package their finest quality herbs and spices in small glass bottles; consider this type of packaging as well as price an indication of quality. Store in airtight containers in a cool, dry place.

Several dried seeds from the family Umbelliferae (the carrot family) are not true spices but are complete fruits. These seeds are extremely rich in flavoring oils. Anise, cumin, fennel, parsley, cilantro and caraway are a few members of this family.

Achuete or Achiote: Reddish colored seeds of the annatto tree. Popular in Filipino, East Indian and Latin cooking. Used to add bright yellow coloring to foods. Sometimes used as a substitute for saffron. Annatto water, annatto paste and annatto powder are available in Southeast Asian and Latin markets.

Allspice: Native to Western hemisphere. Dried berry of a tropical evergreen which tastes like a mixture of cinnamon, cloves and nutmeg. Most comes from Jamaica. Available whole or in ground form.

Ao-noriko: Dried, crushed nutty-tasting nori (laver) is used as a seasoning for Japanese-style rice, noodles and other dishes. Sometimes combined with various herbs and spices.

Black Pepper: (piper nigrum) One of the most important and ancient spices in the world. Made from unripened green fruit of the clinging pepper vine, native to India. When dried, fruits ferment and turn black from presence of a natural fungus. White pepper comes from same vine; ripened berries turn red, are soaked and outer skins removed. When dried, these berries turn white. India, the East Indies and Brazil are largest producers.

Cardamon Pods: A member of the ginger family. Indigenous to India and Sri Lanka. Ranks highly in value along with saffron and vanilla. Purchase aromatic natural green cardamon pods for best flavor in Southeast Asian cooking. In Indian cooking, pods are often gently crushed and used whole. Also used in East Indian, Burmese and Thai cooking. Crushed pods are an excellent flavoring additive in hot coffee or hot tea.

Cinnamon: A tan-colored, smooth, delicately flavored tree bark from an evergreen tree in the laurel family. Native to Asia and rarely sold in U.S. Commonly available is stronger-scented cassia, a reddish-brown bark from a related Asian evergreen tree. Cassia is the preferred spice used in Indian, Pakistani, Vietnamese, East Indian and Chinese cooking. Cinnamon is commonly used in stick and ground form in Southeast Asian cooking. Rarely used in sweets. Added to rice and meat dishes, curries and soups.

Cloves: Pungent dried unopened flower buds of an evergreen tree native to Spice Islands of Indonesia. Used as mouth fresheners by court officials in China several hundred years B.C. Clove oil, used today in commercial mouthwash, is valued for anticeptic properties. Oil is believed to prevent spoilage of meats in Southeast Asian curried dishes.

Coriander Seeds: Rich in flavor oils. Botanically classified as complete fruits. Used extensively in Southeast Asian curry seasoning blends. Mild flavor of seeds is completely different from taste of pungent cilantro leaves.

Cumin Seeds: (white cumin) Rich in flavor oils. Tan-colored seeds are botanically classified as complete fruits. Used extensively in whole and ground form in Indian, Pakistani, East Indian and Thai cooking. Cumin is a major ingredient in Indian-style curry seasoning blends as well as in American chili powder. Indian cooking uses stronger flavored whole black cumin seeds.

Curry Powder: Aromatic blend of spices which forms commercial seasoning. Not commonly used throughtout Southesast Asia. Chinese and Japanese cooks use commercial curry powder to prepare curried dishes. Enhance flavor of commercial product by adding additional ground herbs and spices. No single flavor should be discernable.

Fennel Seeds: Rich in flavor oils. Botanically classified as complete fruits. An important seasoning and often used as a breath freshner and digestive in India. Resemble cumin seeds and darker licorice-flavored anise seeds, but are larger than both. Substitute a reduced amount of anise seeds.

Fenugreek Seeds: Square reddish-brown seeds of the green leafy fenugreek plant are a legume. Used as an important seasoning in Indian cooking. Ground form often added to commercial curry powder blends. A popular flavoring additive to imitation maple syrup products.

Five-Spice Powder: A ground spice-mixture which usually includes star anise, cinnamon, Szechuan peppercorns, cloves, fennel and sometimes other spices. Used primarily in Chinese, East Indian and Indian cooking. Purchase in Asian markets or in spice section of supermarket.

Mace: The aril, or thin red membrane which covers nutmeg, separating it from shell. Removed from nutmeg by hand, dried and sold in Asian markets in pieces (blades) or, more commonly, ground. Becomes a golden-orange when dry. Flavor is stronger than nutmeg.

Mustard Seeds: (brassica juncea) Brown seeds commonly used throughout Southeast Asia and in making Chinese mustard. Black seeds used whole or dry-roasted and ground in many Indian dishes such as chutneys, vegetable dishes, pickles, main dishes and raitas or yogurt based salads. Have a slightly bitter flavor when ground; highly desirable in many Indian dishes.

Nutmeg: Fragrant seed of a fruit from an evergreen tree native to Spice Islands of Indonesia. Fruit is candied and sold throughout East India. Outer net-like covering is removed from seeds and ground to form mace. Seeds are dried several weeks in sun. Used in Indian, East Indian and sometimes in Thai cooking. East Indian nutmeg has a more intense flavor than West Indies nutmeg. Grate whole as needed for uncomparable warm, fresh sweet flavor. Graters available at most cookware shops.

Saffron: Stigmas or threads from the flower saffron-crocus sativus. Each contains only three reddish-orange stigmas. Harvested by hand. Estimated as many as 75,000 flowers are needed to produce one pound. World's most costly spice. Top-grade comes from Spain and is harvested in fall. Fine saffron harvested near Kashmir, India. Adds a subtle, distinctive flavor and characteristic golden color to foods. Beware of ground saffron substitutes of marigold, safflower or tumeric. Used extensively in Indian cuisine.

Salt: (sodium chloride) Mined for a flavor enhancer and preservative for foods as early as 6500 B.C. and in China,

2000 years B.C. Kosher, sea and table salt used in Southeast Asian cooking. Kosher salt is half as salty as table salt. Black salt often used in Indian cooking.

Seven-Spice Mixture: (shichimi togarashi) A Japanese spice blend. Usually includes sesame seeds, poppy seeds, powdered sea weed, dried orange peel, ground sansho pepper, ground chili peppers and flax or hemp seeds. Adds zest to many foods including soups, salads and one-pot and noodle dishes.

Star-Anise: Star-shaped fruit of a small evergreen tree in the Magnolia family. Has eight points; each contains a seed. Adds a delicious licorice-flavor to meats, poultry and fish braised in soy sauce. Use whole or wrap broken points in cheesecloth for cooking. Ground form an important ingredient in five-spice powder.

Szechuan Peppercorns: (fagara) Spicy berries from prickly ash tree. Dried and used as a spicy seasoning in China and Chinese-influenced cuisines. Ground form is blended with salt to make a Chinese table seasoning.

Tumeric: A rhizome from the ginger family with bright yellow flesh. Lacks pungent spiciness of gingerroot. Used commonly as a fabric and food dye in Southeast Asia. Sometimes used as an inexpensive coloring substitute for saffron. Lends color to mustard, pickles, Indian curries, Indonesian rice dishes and commercial curry seasoning blends. Available only in ground form.

Chili peppers are available in many forms. In Asian cooking, ripened dried red chilies are used whole, in crushed red flakes or powdered. The Koreans cut dried ripened chilies in long red threads to be used as a garnish for foods as well as to add flavor.

Ground dried red chili pepper or cayenne pepper is made from fiery bird's eye chili, also used for making several kinds of commercial hot sauce. This ground pepper is sometimes called chili powder, not to be confused with the American spice blend also known as chili powder. Fresh bird's eye chilies can be used in Chinese, Thai, Indian and East Indian cuisines. Small one-inch Mexican serrano chilies or larger jalepeño chiles are good substitutes for small Asian chilies and are available in most supermarkets.

The smallest chilies are usually the hottest. Capsaicin is concentrated in the seeds of the chili pepper and especially in the white membranes to which the seeds are attached. Removing them is one method of slightly diffusing hot chilies.

THE ORIENTAL PANTRY

Efficiency in the oriental kitchen results from a concise understanding of foods and basic cooking principals, and from a well-stocked larder. The latter might easily be considered the oriental cook's best friend. The concept of the pantry, or place to store provisions, can be expanded to include the refrigerator and freezer. Within this chapter, you will find a collection of master recipes you will draw upon time and time again.

Some recipes, such as Basic Cooked White Rice, page 22, and Sushi Rice, page 23, are of such importance they are eaten as a primary food throughout Asia and can stand on their own. The importance of rice as a staple food in the Asian culture can not be overstated. Although foodstuffs and seasonings may vary, rice is the primary grain eaten in almost every area of the Far East. In China, long-grain rice is considered "fan" while all the vegetable and protein dishes are considered as a minor partner or "ts'ai." But only when these are served together is a meal considered well-balanced.

Food staples eaten in the Far East depend largely upon the available natural resources of each country. The choices vary greatly. India, Malaysia, Indonesia and the Philippine Islands are several countries which share a natural resource of coconut palms. Light Coconut Milk, page 21, is the dairy substitute of Southeast Asia and an indispensable staple in the diets of the people of these countries. China, Japan and Korea do not share the use of this resource or that of dairy products to any great extent except in the regions of Outer Mongolia. As adults, this group of Asians have trouble digesting the enzyme lactase which breaks down lactose, an enzyme found in milk with the potential to cause tremendous digestive upsets.

Besides, in part due to lack of grazing land, these countries prefer to rely on soybean products which yield comparable nutrition at far more economical cost. In Pakistan and India where cows and buffalos thrive and are considered sacred, dairy products are enjoyed in the daily diet. A widely used cooking fat is called Ghee, page 25.

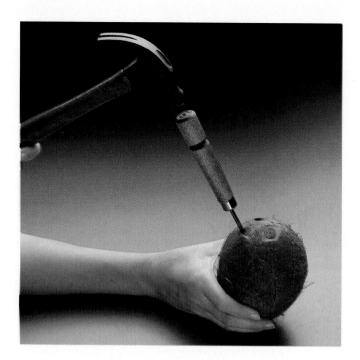

To prepare **Rich Coconut Milk**, *punch holes in the coconut using an icepick and a hammer. This relieves the pressure buildup inside the coconut when it is baked in a preheated oven.*

Dairy Coconut Cream

Chilled and whipped in soft peaks, this delicate coconut-flavored cream can be used as a topping for a variety of favorite desserts. Unwhipped, it can be substituted for plain whipping cream in many recipes.

2 cups whipping cream
1 cup freshly ground coconut or unsweetened shredded dried coconut.

In a medium-size bowl, combine whipping cream and coconut. Cover and refrigerate 24 hours. Strain into a medium-size bowl through a fine strainer lined with several layers of cheesecloth. Gather ends of cheesecloth and squeeze out every drop of coconut cream. Discard coconut grounds. Chill cream until needed. Makes about 2 cups.

VARIATION
To whip cream for a dessert topping, fold in 2 to 3 tablespoons sifted powdered sugar when soft peaks begin to form or substitute 1 cup sweetened flaked dried coconut for fresh or unsweetened dried coconut. Taste for sweetness; add more powdered sugar, if desired.

Rich Coconut Milk

The coconut is a seed from a fruit found on the coconut palm, a food plant valued since antiquity. It is widely believed the coconut palm originated somewhere in the Malayan archipelago. Coconut milk is an important cooking ingredient throughout Southeast Asia; it is used in curries, desserts, beverages and for cooking rice. Coconut milk isn't the clear liquid found inside the mature brown coconut seed. It must be extracted from the white flesh by grinding it with milk or water. Rich Coconut Milk is made with milk from the first pressing of the grated coconut.

1 average-size coconut filled with liquid when shaken
About 2-1/4-cups whole or low-fat milk

Preheat oven to 350F(175C). Using an icepick and a hammer, knock holes in eyes of coconut. Drain coconut water into a small bowl and reserve. In a small baking pan, bake coconut in preheated oven 12 to 15 minutes or until hot. Do not overcook or flesh will be dry. In sink or on newspapers, crack coconut open by tapping center with a hammer. Remove white flesh. Trim away dark outer skin, if desired. Cut flesh in 1/2-inch pieces.

Pour reserved coconut water into a large measuring cup. Add enough milk to make 3 cups. In a medium-size saucepan, heat liquid over low heat until hot. In a blender or food processor fitted with the steel blade, process flesh until coarsely ground. With machine running, slowly pour in hot liquid. Blend until coconut is finely ground. Pour coconut mixture into a medium-size bowl. Cool to room temperature.

Strain milk into a medium-size bowl through a fine strainer lined with several layers of cheesecloth. Gather ends of cheesecloth and squeeze out every drop of coconut milk. Discard coconut grounds. Refrigerate milk up to 3 days. Freeze for longer storage. A layer of coconut cream will rise to top of first pressing; reblend into milk or spoon off for other uses. Makes 2-3/4 to 3 cups.

VARIATIONS

To prepare *Light Coconut Milk*, substitute water for milk.

Substitute 2 cups unsweetened dried coconut for fresh coconut. Bring 3-1/2 cups whole or low-fat milk or water to a simmer over low heat. Combine milk and coconut. Let stand until cool. Strain as directed above. Discard coconut grounds. Refrigerate or freeze milk. Makes about 3 cups.

To obtain a second pressing of coconut milk, heat 2 cups milk or water with coconut grounds. Strain as directed above. Makes about 2 cups.

Good quality commercially canned or frozen coconut milk are fine substitutes for Rich Coconut Milk which is made with milk. Select brands from Thailand or the Philippine Islands. Canned milks are often similar to Light Coconut Milk. Both canned milk and Light Coconut Milk are made with water and are interchangeable in use. Reblend canned and thawed frozen coconut milk after opening. Use full strength or dilute with water by a third, depending on intended use.

Warning! Don't forget to pierce a hole in two of the eyes of the coconut before heating it in the oven. The first time I made coconut milk, I almost launched the coconut into space. The pressure buildup inside the coconut was so great, it simply disappeared when my hammer made contact with the hard outer shell. No problem locating the coconut though; seconds later it crash-landed into a metal garage door.

Crème Fraîche

Everyone should keep a pot of this exquisite-tasting, thick, ripened cream on hand. It becomes a mildly tangy, delicious dessert topping when whipped. Use Crème Fraîche to enrich plain yogurt when making Indian yogurt salads. Stir in some reconstituted Japanese horseradish (wasabi) to make a wonderful sauce for beef or seafood. Use Crème Fraîche any time in place of whipping cream or sour cream. It keeps well and won't separate in cooking. If you prefer a tangier taste, increase sour cream up to one cup. Use only rich pasturized cream; ultrapasteurized cream will not thicken.

1 cup whipping cream
1/2 cup dairy sour cream

In a small saucepan, blend whipping cream and sour cream with a whisk. Heat to 90F (30C) over low heat. Do not allow mixture to become hotter or culture will be inhibited and cream will not thicken. Pour into a warm sterilized glass jar or bowl; cover lightly. Store in a dark place 8 to 12 hours or until cream ripens and becomes thick. Refrigerate after ripening. Cream will continue to slightly thicken. Refrigerate 24 hours for best flavor. Makes 1-1/2 cups.

Basic Cooked White Rice

Historians have traced rice to a plant called "newaree" grown in India 3,000 years B.C. Cooked white rice is the primary food served at any meal throughout most of Southeast Asia. Other dishes are intended to merely enhance the natural taste of rice. Only in Northern India and Northern China does wheat consumption take precedence in the rice-bowl culture. Li Li Weng, ancient Chinese scholar, said "True flavors cannot be counterfeited; no cook has been foolish enough to recreate the flavor of plain rice. If anyone doubts the real flavor of things, let him eat plain rice." (Photo on page 119.)

2 cups white long-grain rice
3 cups bottled spring water or tap water

Rinse rice in a large bowl of cool water, removing any foreign material. Pour off milky water. Continue rinsing until water runs clear. Drain in a fine strainer. In a medium-size saucepan, combine rice and water; soak 30 minutes. Bring rice and water to a boil; continue boiling 30 seconds. Reduce heat to lowest setting. Simmer, tightly covered, 15 minutes. Remove from heat and let stand, covered and undisturbed, 10 minutes.

Carefully break up rice with a dampened Japanese rice paddle or large spoon. Remove rice as needed to a serving bowl; keep remainder covered in saucepan until needed. Makes about 6 cups.

VARIATION
To prepare medium-grain or short-grain rice, decrease water to 2-1/2 cups. Makes about 5-1/2 cups.

Sushi Rice

Japan

Sushi rice is cooked short-grain rice seasoned with a sweet-sour-salty dressing. It should have a firmer bite than regular cooked rice, so the amount of water is reduced. If you don't own a traditional Japanese rice-mixing tub, use a shallow wooden salad bowl with no garlicky or onion odors. Pourous wood has a long memory! You can use a large glass or pottery bowl. I have noticed handsome wooden handcrafted tubs in Scandanavian import shops in shapes similar to Japanese rice tubs. They might make an excellent substitute. Fanning the rice imparts an attractive sheen as it cools. It is fun to have a partner help with the fanning while you are dressing the rice. In Japan I purchased a handy little pink electric fan to do the job for me!

2 cups white short-grain rice
2-1/3 cups bottled spring water or tap water
1 (3-inch) piece dried kelp (konbu), if desired

Sweet & Sour Dressing:
1/4 cup rice vinegar
2 tablespoons sugar
1 tablespoon Japanese sweet rice wine (mirin)
1 tablespoon sake
1-1/2 teaspoons salt

Rinse rice in a large bowl of cool water, removing any foreign material. Pour off milky water. Continue rinsing until water runs clear. Drain in a fine strainer. In a large saucepan or rice cooker, combine rice, water and kelp, if desired; soak 30 minutes. Bring rice and water to a boil; continue boiling 30 seconds. If using kelp, remove just before water boils. Reduce heat to lowest setting. Simmer, tightly covered, 15 minutes. Remove from heat and let stand, covered and undisturbed, 10 minutes.

Prepare Sweet & Sour Dressing. Rinse a cedar rice-mixing tub (hangiri) or other container with water. Rice should be hot when dressing is added. Using a dampened wooden rice paddle or spatula, gently scoop hot rice into tub. Hold paddle over rice. Sprinkle a little dressing onto rice paddle, letting it drip onto rice. Do not add entire amount at 1 time. It may not be needed. Toss rice with a gentle cutting and tossing motion. Do not crush grains. As dressing is added, constantly fan rice to cool and remove moisture. Continue sprinkling in dressing, a little at a time. Use only as much as rice will absorb without becoming mushy.

Cover with a damp cloth; do not refrigerate. Rice is best used within 3 to 4 hours. Or cover with a damp cloth and use within 12 to 16 hours. Makes about 6 cups.

Sweet & Sour Dressing:
In a small saucepan, combine all ingredients. Cook, stirring constantly, over low heat until sugar is dissolved. Cool to room temperature. Makes about 1/2 cup.

Dry Roasted Sesame Seeds *Southeast Asia*

Throughout Southeast Asia, sesame seeds are added to sauces, batters, savory dishes, breads and sweet snacks. They are ground to make seasoning mixtures and seasoning pastes. Dry roasting enhances the flavor of sesame seeds. After roasting, crush slightiy to release their fragrant oils. They give foods a warm, nutty taste. It is best to roast sesame seeds as needed for maximum freshness. Use attractive hulled white sesame seeds when appearance is important; otherwise, tan-colored, unhulled sesame seeds are fine.

Hulled or unhulled white sesame seeds or black sesame seeds, as needed

In a small skillet, heat sesame seeds, stirring constantly, over medium-high heat. When seeds begin to pop, they are almost ready. Watch carefully at this point; they can burn quickly. Let white sesame seeds darken to a medium golden-brown. Color is not a good indicator when roasting black sesame seeds; toast until fragrant.

Egg Crepe

Use this tasty thin sheet of egg to add color, flavor and texture to Asian dishes. Egg Crepes are commonly cut in decorative matchstick julienne strips.

> **1 jumbo egg or 2 small eggs**
> **1/8 teaspoon salt**
> **1/4 teaspoon sesame seed oil**
> **1/2 teaspoon sugar**
> **2 teaspoons water**

In a small bowl, beat all ingredients with a fork. Heat a 9- or 10-inch nonstick skillet over medium-high heat. Wipe skillet with a paper towel dipped into vegetable oil. Pour egg mixture into oiled skillet. Swirl skillet so egg mixture covers bottom of pan in a thin sheet. Reduce heat to low. Cook egg crepe 30 seconds or until set. Remove from heat. Carefully turn crepe over; cook 30 seconds more. Turn crepe out of skillet. Cool and cut as desired. Makes 1 (9- or 10-inch) crepe.

Indonesian Soy Sauce *Indonesia*

Use this sauce as an approximation of the rich sweet soy sauce found in Indonesia. It will add a gentle sweetness and a hint of spice to many of your Indonesian and Malaysian foods including sauces, noodle and rice dishes and curries.

> **1/2 cup medium Japanese soy sauce**
> **1/2 cup Thin Caramel Syrup, page 27**
> **1/4 cup molasses**
> **1 (1/8-inch) slice fresh gingerroot, smashed**
> **1/4 teaspoon red pepper (cayenne)**
> **1/2 whole star anise (4 points)**

Combine all ingredients in a small glass jar. Let stand 2 days in a cool place. Remove gingerroot and star anise. Flavor of soy sauce is enhanced after several days. Refrigerate up to several months. Makes about 1-1/4 cups.

*To prepare **Ghee**, simmer the unsalted butter until the butterfat separates from the milk-solids and the milk-solids turn golden-brown. Pour off the clear butterfat.*

Ghee is an Indian-style clarified butter.

Ghee

India

Usli ghee, or pure butterfat, is one of the primary fats used for cooking in India. It is made by simmering unsalted butter in a saucepan until the golden butterfat separates from the whitish milk solids. To make ghee, the butter requires long, low simmering to evaporate moisture in the milk solids and to give it a characteristic rich, nutty flavor. You can steep different herbs or spices in ghee to create a variety of flavors. Ghee is available already made in Indian and Southeast Asian markets, but homemade tastes better.

2 pounds top-quality unsalted butter

In a heavy medium-size saucepan, melt butter over lowest possible setting. Cook 45 minutes to 1 hour or until butterfat separates from milk solids and milk solids turn golden-brown. Watch carefully; occasionally gently skim through browned milk solids to be sure they are not burning. Cool slightly. When milk solids have sunk to bottom, strain clear butterfat through a fine strainer lined with several layers of cheesecloth into a container. Cover tightly and store in refrigerator or a cool place 3 to 4 weeks. Makes about 2-3/4 cups.

Crispy Fried Shallots

Indonesia, Malaysia, India

When shallots, onions and garlic are fried until crispy and golden-brown, their sharp bite is mellowed and they take on a slightly sweet taste from the caramelization of natural sugars. Use these fried crispy aromatic vegetables as toppings for rice and other dishes.

12 to 15 shallots, sliced paper thin
1/2 teaspoon salt
3 tablespoons vegetable oil

Spread sliced shallots on several layers of paper towels. Sprinkle with salt. Let stand 10 minutes or until moisture is released. Gently press out remaining moisture; pat dry. In a large skillet, heat oil over medium-low heat until hot. Fry shallots, stirring constantly, 20 minutes or until golden-brown and crispy. Increase heat slightly toward end of cooking time. Drain on paper towels. Store in an airtight container. Recrisp fried shallots in a preheated 350F (175C) oven until hot. Makes about 1/2 cup.

VARIATIONS

To make *Crispy Fried Onions,* substitute 2 large onions, thinly sliced, for shallots. Increase salt to 2 teaspoons and vegetable oil to 1/4 cup. Increase frying time to 40 minutes or until onions are crispy and medium-brown. Stir often to ensure even browning and to prevent burning.

To make *Crispy Fried Garlic,* substitute 15 large garlic cloves, thinly sliced, for shallots. Decrease cooking time to 3 to 4 minutes. Do not allow garlic to burn or taste will be bitter.

Gingery Chicken Stock

Southeast Asian

Use this excellent quality chicken stock as a hearty flavor base for Southeast Asian soups and other dishes. Make ahead and refrigerate or freeze until needed.

1 (3- to 3-1/2-lb.) broiler-fryer
3 to 4 pounds chicken parts, such as backs, necks or wings
5 green onions or 2 leeks, cut in half, well rinsed
1 (1-1/2-inch) piece fresh gingerroot, thinly sliced
About 5 quarts bottled spring water or tap water

Rinse chicken and chicken parts under cool running water. Remove fat pads. Place all ingredients in a stockpot over medium-high heat. When stock bubbles, reduce heat to low and simmer, uncovered, 30 minutes. Occasionally skim off foam. Do not boil or stir. If desired, remove breast and thigh meat from whole chicken after 30 minutes; reserve for another use. Continue simmering stock 1-1/2 to 2 hours. Add water as needed.
  Strain into a larger pan; discard solids. For greater clarity, strain stock again through a strainer lined with several layers of dampened cheesecloth. Cool stock, uncovered, 1 hour. Makes about 5 quarts.

HINT
Gingery Chicken Stock can be refrigerated up to 3 days. Skim off surface fat and bring to a boil before using. Small amounts of defatted stock can be frozen 1 to 2 months. Stock flavor can be concentrated by boiling and reducing it by a third to a half. Salt to taste when using.

Thin Caramel Syrup

Viet Nam

This smooth amber syrup is a staple in Vietnamese cooking. It adds a rich caramel flavor to foods, as well as character and sweetness. Try it in Caramelized Lemon Shrimp, page 88-89, and in Indonesian Soy Sauce, page 24. Keep on hand to use as an instant sweet-topping or for many other cooking purposes.

> **1/2 cup sugar**
> **3 tablespoons water**
> **1/2 cup hot water**

In a copper sugar-pot or small heavy skillet, combine sugar and 3 tablespoons water over low heat. Use water to wash down sugar from pan sides. When sugar has dissolved, increase heat to medium-high. When mixture is bubbly, water will begin to evaporate and sugar will begin to melt. Cook sugar until completely melted in a medium-brown syrup.

Remove sugar-pot from heat. Sugar will continue to cook and can darken and burn easily. Carefully add part of hot water; mixture will bubble furiously. With a long wooden-handled spoon, stir in remaining water. Return pan to heat; cook 3 to 4 minutes to reduce and thicken syrup slightly. Stir to dissolve any crystalized sugar pieces. Cool and store in an airtight container in refrigerator or in a cool place. Makes about 1/2 cup.

Basic Tender Butter Pastry

When making pastry, a large amount of fat is cut into the flour to coat and inhibit development of gluten, the elastic protein substance which is formed in flour when water is added. Some gluten development is necessary to form the structure of pastry, too much and the pastry is tough. Butter combined with a small amount of malleable, solid vegetable shortening works best for making pastry which is easy to handle, stays tender after baking and tastes good. Adding a small amount of acid such as vinegar or lemon juice helps tenderize the gluten strands, making the pastry easier to handle. Just add one teaspoon of acid-based liquid to the iced water called for in your recipe. Keep pastry well-chilled for easy handling. Prepare and refrigerate pastry two to three days ahead. This saves time during last minute baking and gives you, as well as your delicious pastry, time to relax!

> **4 cups all-purpose flour, lightly spooned into cup**
> **1-1/2 teaspoons salt**
> **1/2 cup chilled vegetable shortening**
> **1-1/4 cups frozen unsalted butter, cut in 1-tablespoon pieces**
> **1/2 cup iced water**

Place flour in a food processor fitted with the steel blade. Add salt; process 5 to 10 seconds. Add vegetable shortening to flour; process until mixture resembles coarsley ground cornmeal. Distribute frozen butter pieces evenly around top of flour mixture. Cut butter partially into flour using 10 to 15 short bursts of power. Remove lid; sprinkle 3 tablespoons of iced water over flour. Replace lid; activate processor with short bursts of power. Continue processing, adding just enough water to bind flour and fat into moist clumps. Do not allow mixture to form a ball or pastry will be tough.

Turn out pastry onto plastic wrap. Pat mixture in a mound. Using heel of hand, gently press moist clumps in a cohesive flattened round shape. Wrap in plastic wrap; chill at least 1 hour. Roll out and cut chilled dough as desired. Makes enough pastry for 2 (9- to 10-inch) one-crust shells or 1 large two-crust shell.

> **HINT**
> *If your food processor has a small workbowl, it is best to divide ingredients and make 1/2 recipe of pastry at a time. Pastry can be frozen.*

Golden Flaky Pastry

This Malaysian-influenced tender flaky pastry is made following principals similar to those used in making classic French puff pastry, but in far less time and with half the work. To create such flakiness, pieces of cold fat must be layered and folded into the dough rather than being cut in as for a super-tender pastry. You can use this pastry as a substitute for "shao bing," the Northern Chinese layered pastry made by rolling balls of oil-dough inside flattened balls of softer water-dough. This pastry is excellent for use in a variety of Asian recipes such as Curried Lamb Crescents with Pine Nuts & Apricot Sauce, page 44, or Teahouse Golden Custard Tartlets, page 148.

1 large egg yolk
1 tablespoon sugar
1 teaspoon salt
1 teaspoon fresh lime juice or lemon juice
1/4 cup plus 1 tablespoon iced water
3 drops yellow food coloring, if desired
1/4 cup lard or vegetable shortening
2 cups sifted all-purpose flour
1/2 cup plus 2 tablespoons ice-cold unsalted butter
Additional flour

In a small bowl, beat egg yolk with a fork. Stir in sugar, salt, lime juice and iced water. Add food coloring, if desired. Chill mixture in freezer 5 minutes. In a medium-size bowl, rub lard into flour with hands until mixture resembles bread crumbs. Cut butter in 1/2-inch cubes. Separate cubes; add to flour. Using hands, toss butter cubes in flour, coating them completely. Stir in 1 to 2 tablespoons of chilled egg yolk mixture at a time, trying not to break up shape of butter cubes. Add only enough egg yolk mixture to bind flour and butter in a cohesive mixture.

Turn out dough onto plastic wrap. If necessary, dust with a small amount of flour to prevent sticking. Press dough in an 8'' x 5-1/2'' rectangle about 3/4-inch thick. Wrap in plastic wrap; chill 1 hour. On a lightly floured surface, place dough with a short end near you. Roll out dough to a 12'' x 8'' rectangle, patting edges evenly in shape. Fold up bottom 1/3 of dough just above center. Fold down top third over bottom fold to resemble a letter; dough has now been folded in a single fold. Turn dough 90 degrees counterclockwise, so edge of top fold faces right. Roll out dough again in a 12'' x 8'' rectangle. Fold in a single fold as directed above. Wrap dough in plastic wrap; chill 1 to 3 hours.

On a lightly floured surface, place dough so top edge faces right. Roll out dough; fold in a single fold as directed above. Give dough a third turn. Roll out dough for fourth time; give dough a fourth and final turn. Cold dough may be slightly difficult to roll at this point. Do not allow pastry to warm up for easier rolling; soft butter will press out, ruining dough. Wrap dough; chill at least 2 hours or up to 2 days.

To roll out dough for cutting, place in position for fourth turn with edge of top fold facing right. Roll out dough to a 15-inch square. Cut as directed in selected recipe or use as desired. Makes about 1 pound dough.

HINT
This dough freezes well for longer storage.

*To prepare **Golden Flaky Pastry**, add small cubes of cold butter to the flour and lard mixture to create flakiness.*

Roll the pastry dough to an 8'' x 5-1/2'' rectangle and fold the dough in thirds to resemble a letter.

Golden Egg-Puff Paste

Baking pâté à chou, or cream puff paste, is like performing a magic act in the oven. Dough expansion comes from the addition of whole eggs to the cooked flour paste. Eggs create steam which act as a leavening agent. Slightly cool the cooked flour paste before beating in eggs. If mixture is too hot and the eggs coagulate, interference with the "high rise" act which takes place in the oven will occur.

> **1/4 cup plus 2 tablespoons unsalted butter**
> **3/4 cup plus 2 tablespoons water**
> **2 tablespoons Rich Coconut Milk, page 21, milk or water**
> **1 teaspoon sugar**
> **1/4 generous teaspoon ground tumeric**
> **1/4 teaspoon freshly grated nutmeg**
> **1/2 teaspoon salt**
> **1 cup plus 2 tablespoons all-purpose flour**
> **4 large eggs, room temperature**

In a medium-size saucepan, heat butter, water and Rich Coconut Milk over medium-high heat. Stir sugar, tumeric, nutmeg and salt into mixture. When liquid comes to a boil, remove from heat. Quickly add flour while beating firmly with a wooden spoon. Mixture will leave sides of pan and form a ball around spoon. Reduce heat; stir dough briskly over heat 45 seconds to dry slightly. Remove pan from heat.

Spoon 2 or 3 portions of dough into a medium-size bowl or into a food processor fitted with the steel blade. Cool 5 minutes; dough will cool faster when divided. Add 1 egg at a time to warm dough, blending thoroughly after each addition. Paste should be smooth and shiny. For greatest expansion, use paste immediately. To hold at room temperature up to 1 hour, place plastic wrap on top of paste. Makes about 2-1/4 cups.

Rich Egg Dough

This golden, tender egg dough is made quickly in the food processor, and features the use of instant egg custard mix in place of fresh eggs. It's easy and fun to make and delicious! This rich dense dough doesn't like to be hurried while rising so allow plenty of time. Steaming is the best method of cooking; it keeps it moist and tender, never drying. This dough is interchangeable with Basic Chinese Yeast Bread, Chinese-Style Steamed Sandwich Buns, page 116.

      2 (1/4-oz.) packages active dry yeast (2 tablespoons)
      1 cup warm water (110F/45C)
      1/4 cup plus 1 tablespoon sugar
      3-1/2 to 4 cups all-purpose flour
      1 (3-oz.) package golden egg custard mix (1/2 cup plus 1 generous tablespoon)
      1 teaspoon salt
      1/4 cup unsalted butter, cut in small pieces
      Vegetable oil

Lightly oil a large bowl. In a medium-size bowl, dissolve yeast in water; stir in 1 tablespoon of sugar. Let stand until foamy, 5 to 10 minutes. In a food processor fitted with the steel blade, blend in remaining sugar, 3 cups of flour, custard mix and salt. Add butter; process briefly to cut into flour mixture. With processor running, pour yeast mixture through feed tube; process about 20 seconds. Add 1/2 cup of flour; process until mixture forms a ball. If processor begins to slow down, add remaining flour in small amounts until processor is able to handle sticky mixture and process normally. Process dough nonstop 60 seconds. If desired, divide dough in half and process each half separately 60 seconds.

    After kneading, remove steel blade from processsor. Oil hands lightly; remove dough. On a lightly floured surface, knead dough 15 seconds. Form dough in a rounded shape; rub surface lightly with oil. Place in oiled bowl; cover with a damp kitchen towel. Let dough rise until doubled, about 1-1/2 hours. Punch dough down; reshape. Let dough rise again until doubled, about 1 hour. Punch dough down; knead briefly 10 seconds. Form in shapes and steam as directed in selected recipe. Makes about 2 pounds dough.

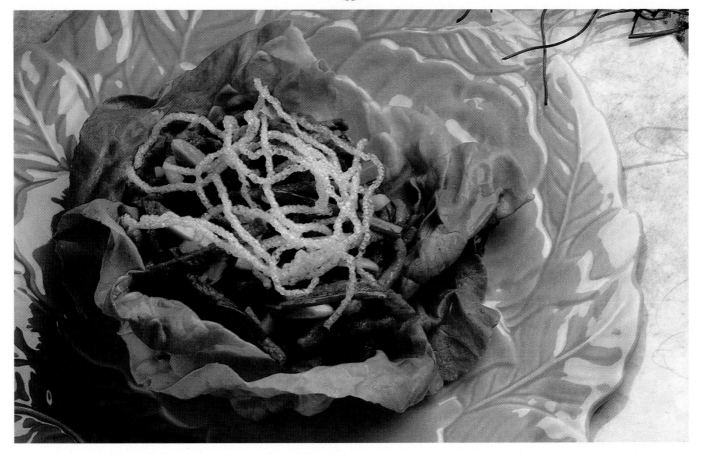

APPETIZERS

By definition, appetizers are "tasty foods that stimulate the appetite, usually served before a meal." Many foods which qualify as Asian appetizers can play a dual-role. Double the recipes if necessary, and serve them as a main course within the context of another meal. Appetizers are rarely served before family meals in Asia. Several kinds might be prepared and served for a brief period before a special dinner party, the actual amount depending on the occasion and the number of guests attending. However, the focus of the evening will be on the main portion of the meal. In Japan, appetizers and similiar little snacks have many names depending on how and where they are served. "Zensai" are small elegant portions of flavorful foods which are intended to awaken the taste buds for the flavors in the meal which is to come.

In some Asian countries, men frequent special drinking establishments to socialize and enjoy the many types of appetizer foods such as the salad-like dish Szechuan Marinated Vegetables, page 132. In Japan, these are called "tsukidashi" or "sakizuke" which indicates they are foods to enjoy with sake.

Thinly sliced cold cuts such as Orange-Flavored Beef, page 41, have long been an appetizer favorite on the Chinese party table. Prepare this dish ahead of time, then thinly slice it when cold. Arrange on a serving platter in a decorative pattern, alone or with other appetizers. The flavors of the spiced beef keep getting better and better!

If you are planning several appetizers for a party, why not select your recipes, then try them out on the family first as a trial run. Don't plan on making too many dishes if you are planning a special dinner. Coordinate dishes so they will all be prepared in advance.

Shanghaied Chicken Nuggets

China

Chicken nuggets have never tasted so good! Prepared Chinese-style, these crispy morsels make a great appetizer with your favorite dipping sauce or can be served as a main dish. Darker thigh meat is economical and stays tender and moist during frying. The delicate sesame seed batter is excellent for coating pieces of seafood or vegetables such as mushrooms, eggplant and tofu. The special Japanese-style bread-crumb coating helps keep the chicken bites crispy long after frying.

4 chicken thighs, skinned, boned, cut in 1-inch cubes
1 tablespoon hoisin sauce
1 tablespoon dry white wine
1 tablespoon medium Chinese or Japanese soy sauce
1 teaspoon grated fresh gingerroot
6 cups peanut or vegetable oil for deep-frying
2 cups Japanese-style bread crumbs (panko)
1 recipe Plum-Brandy Sauce, page 136, Chinese Red Hot Sauce, page 137, or Apricot Sauce, Curried Lamb Crescents with Pine Nuts & Apricot Sauce, page 44

Sesame Seed Batter:
1/3 cup cake flour
1/3 cup potato starch or cornstarch
1/2 teaspoon baking powder
3/4 teaspoon salt
1/2 cup plus 2 teaspoons sparkling water or tap water
1 teaspoon vegetable oil
2 teaspoons hulled white sesame seeds

In a medium-size bowl, combine chicken, hoisin sauce, wine, soy sauce and gingerroot. Marinate at least 30 minutes or overnight. Prepare Sesame Seed Batter. In a wok or shallow heavy saucepan, heat oil to 360F (180C) or until a 1-inch cube of bread turns golden-brown in 60 seconds. While oil is heating, drain chicken. Dip chicken pieces into Sesame Seed Batter; coat with bread crumbs. Fry several pieces at a time 2 to 3 minutes or until crispy and golden-brown. Drain on a wire rack. Serve with sauce for dipping. Makes 6 to 8 servings.

Sesame Seed Batter:
In a small bowl, combine flour, potato starch, baking powder and salt. Stir in water, oil and sesame seeds. Combine just until smooth. Makes about 1 cup.

VARIATION
Wrap small strips of bacon around chicken pieces and secure with wooden picks before coating with batter. Remove wooden picks after frying.

HINT
Chicken bites can be prepared up to 1 hour ahead. Reheat in a preheated 375F (190C) oven 5 minutes or until hot and crisp.

Sesame-Tofu Meatballs

Korea

Korean foods are robust and highly seasoned. They are characterized by the liberal use of hot red peppers, green onions, garlic and sesame seeds. Used in combination, they add character and zip to poultry and meat dishes. Tofu is a powerhouse of nutrients. As a meat extender in ground-meat mixtures, tofu adds extra nutrition and helps to keep them moist and light. The appearance and mild tofu flavor are imperceptible. Try adding tofu to your next batch of hamburgers, a tasty way to enjoy eating beef and, at the same time, cut down on cholesterol and saturated fats.

1 teaspoon Dry Roasted Sesame Seeds, page 24
1 recipe Spicy Soy Sauce Dip, page 140
1 recipe Cranberry-Orange Dipping Sauce, page 137
1 tablespoon vegetable oil
1 tablespoon unsalted butter or margarine

Meatball Mixture:
8 ounces silken or regular Japanese-style tofu (about 1 cup), well rinsed
1 pound lean ground pork or beef
1 tablespoon Dry Roasted Sesame Seeds, page 24
1 heaping teaspoon finely minced fresh gingerroot
2 large garlic cloves, finely minced
1 tablespoon dry white wine
2 tablespoons medium Japanese soy sauce
1/2 teaspoon sesame seed oil
1 teaspoon ground Korean hot red peppers or 1/2 teaspoon red pepper (cayenne)
1/2 teaspoon sugar
1/2 teaspoon salt, if desired
Black pepper to taste

Stir Dry Roasted Sesame Seeds into Spicy Soy Sauce Dip. Prepare Meatball Mixture. In a large skillet, heat oil and butter over medium-high heat until hot. Add meatballs and fry 8 to 10 minutes, turning often to brown on all sides. Drain well. Serve with Spicy Soy Sauce Dip and Cranberry-Orange Dipping Sauce. Makes 8 servings.

Meatball Mixture:
Pat rinsed tofu dry. In a medium-size bowl, mash tofu well. Add remaining ingredients; blend until well combined. Form in meatballs using 1 tablespoon of mixture per meatball.

VARIATION
To prepare *Cranberry-Glazed Sesame-Tofu Meatballs*, roll meatballs in 1/3 cup cornstarch before frying. Sauté until brown. Combine 3/4 cup cranberry juice cocktail, 1/4 cup freshly squeezed orange juice and 1 teaspoon freshly grated orange peel. Add to meatballs, cover and simmer until done. Juice should reduce to a slightly thickened glaze.

HINT
Meatballs can be prepared 1 day ahead. Cool, cover and refrigerate until needed. Reheat on a foil-lined pan in a preheated oven (350F/175C) 10 to 12 minutes or until hot. Meatballs reheat well in a microwave oven.

Shrimp & Pork Rissoles   *Malaysia*

Rissoles are fried spring rolls, Malaysian-style. The filling contains cubes of cooked yam which add a delicious sweet touch. The velvety golden wrappers are scented and colored with tumeric. When coated with dried Japanese bread crumbs for frying, they take on a special texture which stays crunchy for hours. Diced hearts of palm would be a nice addition to this recipe.

> **3 large eggs, slightly beaten**
> **4 cups peanut or vegetable oil for deep-frying**
> **4 cups Japanese-style bread crumbs (panko)**
> **1 recipe Garlic & Vinegar Dipping Sauce, page 140**
>
> *Shrimp & Pork Filling:*
> **1/2 pound fresh medium-size shrimp, peeled, deveined, finely chopped**
> **1 tablespoon dry white wine**
> **1/2 teaspoon cornstarch**
> **1 tablespoon vegetable oil**
> **1 medium-size red Bermuda onion, cut in half, thinly sliced**
> **3 large garlic cloves, minced**
> **1/2 pound ground pork**
> **1 cup raw yam or sweet potato cubes, cut in 1/2-inch squares, parboiled until**
> **crisp-tender**
> **1/4 pound fresh young green beans, blanched 3 minutes, cut in 1-1/2-inch**
> **julienne strips**
> **1/2 cup chicken stock or as needed**
> **1 cup shredded tender young cabbage leaves**
> **1 cup fresh bean sprouts**
> **Salt and black pepper to taste**
> **2 tablespoons Indonesian Soy Sauce, page 24, or medium Japanese soy sauce**
> **1 tablespoon sugar**
> **1 teaspoon cornstarch**
>
> *Golden Egg Wrappers:*
> **1 cup all-purpose flour**
> **2 tablespoons cornstarch**
> **4 large eggs**
> **2 tablespoons vegetable oil**
> **1/2 teaspoon salt**
> **1/2 teaspoon ground tumeric**
> **1-1/4 cups water**

Prepare Shrimp & Pork Filling and Golden Egg Wrappers. To form rissoles, place 1 wrapper on a flat surface. On upper third section of each wrapper, spoon 2 to 3 tablespoons of filling; form filling in an elongated shape. Fold sides of wrapper over ends of filling. Fold top portion of wrapper down to cover filling; continue rolling until filling is enclosed. Seal edges of wrapper with a small amount of beaten egg. Repeat with remaining wrappers and filling.

In a wok or shallow heavy saucepan, heat oil to 360F (180C) or until a 1-inch cube of bread turns golden-brown in 60 seconds. Dip each rissole into beaten egg, then coat completely with bread crumbs. Fry 2 to 3 rissoles in hot oil 3 to 4 minutes or until coating is crispy and medium golden-brown. Drain on paper towels. Serve with Garlic & Vinegar Dipping Sauce. Makes 20 to 22 rissoles.

To prepare **Shrimp & Pork Rissoles***, swirl the batter in a hot pan and cook until the wrapper is set.*

Spoon the cooked pork, shrimp and yam filling onto the Golden Egg Wrappers. Roll and coat the rolls with Japanese-style bread crumbs.

Shrimp & Pork Filling:
In a small bowl, combine shrimp, wine and cornstarch. Let stand 10 minutes. In a wok or large skillet, heat oil over medium-high heat. Add onion and garlic; fry 1 minute. Add pork; cook until no longer pink. Break up large pieces. Add yam and green beans. If yam cubes are not tender, add 1/4 cup of chicken stock. Cover and simmer briefly until yams are tender and liquid evaporates. Turn mixture as it cooks.

Drain shrimp; add to pork mixture. Cook 30 seconds. Add cabbage and bean sprouts; cook 1 to 2 minutes more. Add salt and black pepper; sprinkle in soy sauce and sugar. Combine ingredients carefully. In a small bowl, blend remaining chicken stock and cornstarch. Push pork-shrimp mixture away from center of wok. Pour in stock mixture; cook and stir 1 minute or until thickened. Remove filling to a platter; cool before use. Makes about 4 cups filling.

Golden Egg Wrappers:
In a blender or food processor fitted with the steel blade, combine all ingredients. Process until smooth. Pour batter into a medium-size bowl. Cover and let stand 20 minutes. Heat a crepe pan over medium-low heat. If pan is not nonstick, wipe with vegetable oil.

Pour 1/8 cup of batter into pan. Roll pan to thinly coat bottom of pan; wrapper should be 7-inches in diameter. If pan is too hot, batter will not swirl easily to proper size. Cook 30 seconds or until wrapper is set. Turn and cook 30 seconds. Remove from pan. Place on waxed paper. Repeat with remaining batter. Cool completely. Makes 20 to 22 wrappers.

HINTS
Rissoles will remain crisp at room temperature 2 to 3 hours. Reheat in a preheated oven 350F (175C) until hot and crispy.

Cooled Golden Egg Wrappers can be stacked, wrapped and refrigerated overnight.

Shredded Beef & Almonds in Lettuce Cups

China

Japanese miso paste blends happily with the components of this Chinese stir-fry dish, enriching the flavor and adding a rich, somewhat-meaty taste. Prepare a spicy version by adding two to three teaspoons of Szechuan ground bean paste with chilies and garlic from Taiwan. Found in most Asian markets, this piquant sauce adds wonderful character to dishes as well as a touch of heat. The colorful lettuce leaves filled with beef and topped with crisp puffed snow-white noodles create a rather spectacular appetizer or first course. (Photo on page 43.)

1 pound beef round eye steak, flank steak or other beef, partially frozen
3 medium-size dried shiitake mushrooms
1 heaping tablespoon red miso paste
1 tablespoon water
1/3 cup vegetable oil
1/3 cup minced bamboo shoots
1/3 cup minced water chestnuts
6 small green onions, slivered
2 teaspoons finely minced fresh gingerroot
2 large garlic cloves, finely minced
1/3 cup blanched slivered toasted almonds
1/2 teaspoon cornstarch mixed with 2 tablespoons water
10 to 12 fresh Bibb lettuce leaves

Marinade:
3 tablespoons medium Chinese or Japanese soy sauce
2 teaspoons cornstarch
1 tablespoon dry white wine
1 teaspoon sesame seed oil
1/4 teaspoon black pepper
1 teaspoon finely minced fresh gingerroot
1 large garlic clove, finely minced
1 tablespoon water

Crispy Fried Rice Sticks:
1/2 bunch thin (about 1/16-inch-thick) dried rice sticks
6 cups peanut or vegetable oil for deep-frying

Prepare Marinade. With a cleaver or other large sharp knife, slice beef across grain in thin slices. Stack several slices and cut in matchstick shreds about 2-inches long. Repeat with remaining slices. Combine Marinade and beef until beef is coated. Cover and refrigerate at least 2 hours or up to 12 hours. Remove beef from refrigerator 30 minutes before cooking.

   In a medium-size bowl, cover mushrooms with warm water. Soak 30 minutes or until needed. Prepare Crispy Fried Rice Sticks. Squeeze mushrooms dry; cut off and discard tough stems. Cut mushrooms in thin shreds. In a small bowl, thin miso paste with water. Heat a wok or large skillet over high heat. Add 1/2 of oil. When oil is hot, add mushrooms, bamboo shoots, water chestnuts, green onions, gingerroot and garlic. Stir-fry 1 minute. Remove vegetable mixture to a platter.

Wipe wok clean and dry with paper towels; reheat over high heat. Add remaining oil. When oil is almost to smoking point, add beef. Stir-fry 30 seconds. Add thinned miso paste. Continue stir-frying until beef is no longer pink and excess moisture has evaporated. Add vegetable mixture and almonds to beef; combine well. If a glaze is needed, reduce heat sightly. Make a well in center of meat mixture; pour in cornstarch and water. Cook, stirring constantly, 30 seconds or until thickened; combine with beef mixture. Remove to a platter. Spoon beef mixture into lettuce cups. Sprinkle with Crispy Fried Rice Sticks. Serve at once. Makes 10 to 12 appetizer servings or 5 to 6 first course servings.

Marinade:
In a medium-size bowl, combine all ingredients. Makes about 1/3 cup.

Crispy Fried Rice Sticks:
Tear rice sticks in small manageable clusters. In a wok or shallow heavy saucepan, heat oil to 400F (205C) or until a 1-inch cube of bread turns golden-brown in 20 seconds. Drop 1 cluster of rice sticks in hot oil; it should instantly expand in size. With a pair of chopsticks or a Chinese strainer, turn rice sticks over and cook 10 seconds. Drain on paper towels. Repeat with remaining rice stick clusters.

VARIATION
Substitute dried mung bean noodles or bean threads for rice sticks. Cut these tough noodles with kitchen scissors inside a paper bag as they tend to be flyaway.

HINT
Although this dish is cooked just before serving, all preparation can be done in advance. Beef can be cut and marinated hours ahead. Vegetables can be prepared and covered several hours before cooking. Almonds, lettuce leaves and Crispy Fried Rice Sticks can be prepared ahead.

Eating noodles could be considered one of the universal pastimes throughout the Orient. Asians enjoy gathering in a small convivial atmosphere to share good conversation over a plate of delicious noodles. Throughout Asia, one can purchase a variety of noodle dishes from tiny noodle shops, street stalls, tea shops and pushcarts of the mobile noodle vendors. It isn't for certain who really made the first noodle, but we can thank China for the advances in the milling technology which came to China during the Han Dynasty and to all the creative cooks in China who have been "noodling" ever since! Their methods and ideas have greatly influenced cooks throughout all of Asia for centuries.

Steamed Pork & Rice Chrysanthemums   *Japan*

Surprise your guests with a bouquet of edible chrysanthemums. Savory pork patties are partially coated with pastel-coated glutinous rice, then steamed until they " blossom." They are first cousins to the popular Chinese steamed pearl balls. Serve the rice-covered pork balls as appetizers or as part of a multicourse Asian meal. Present them on a beautiful platter garnished with fresh chrysanthemum leaves or in pairs on individual serving plates.

1 cup sweet glutinous rice
2 cups water
2 to 3 drops red food coloring
2 to 3 drops yellow food coloring
1 pound ground pork
1 large egg
2 green onions, finely minced
2 teaspoons sesame seed oil
2 tablespoons medium Japanese soy sauce
2 tablespoons chicken stock or water
2 tablespoons sake
1/2 teaspoon salt
1 generous teaspoon grated fresh gingerroot
1 large garlic clove, finely minced
Fresh chrysanthemum leaves or mint leaves, if desired
1 recipe Spicy Soy Sauce Dip, page 140

In a medium-size bowl, wash rice thoroughly in cool water. Pour off milky water and add fresh water. Continue washing rice and changing water until water is clear. Drain rice and divide between 2 medium-size bowls. Add 1 cup of water to each bowl. Add red food coloring to rice in 1 bowl, yellow food coloring to rice in other bowl. Soak at least 6 hours or overnight.

In a large bowl, combine pork with egg, green onions, sesame seed oil, soy sauce, chicken stock, sake, salt, gingerroot and garlic. Drain each bowl of rice separately into a fine strainer; place each on a separate plate. Form 16 to 18 pork patties, approximately 2-inches in diameter and about 3/4-inch thick. Press tops and sides of 1/2 of patties into pink rice. Press remaining patties into yellow rice.

In a wok or deep pot, bring water to a boil over high heat. Line a steamer tray with a dampened piece of cheesecloth. Put patties on cheesecloth, rice-sides up. Cover and place over boiling water. Reduce heat to medium-high. Steam 30 minutes or until pork is no longer pink inside and rice is tender. Place 1 pink and 1 yellow rice chrysanthemum on each serving plate. Garnish with a chrysanthemum leaf, if desired. Serve with Spicy Soy Sauce Dip. Makes 8 to 10 servings.

VARIATION
Omit food coloring, if desired.

Steamed Pork & Rice Chrysanthemums

Princess Hats

Malaysia

This recipe was inspired by a Malaysian snack I tasted in Hong Kong on the eve of the wedding of the Prince and Princess of Wales. Macadamia nuts are used in the aromatic seasoning paste which flavors the chicken spread. Their rich flavor and oily texture provide a good substitute for hard-to-find kemiri nuts, preferred in Malaysian and Indonesian cuisine. Kemiri nuts are called candle nuts because of the old Malaysian custom of threading and burning them as candles. These appetizers are decorated to resemble tiny hats, the fashion signature of the Princess of Wales. Serve these charming snacks at a Malaysian-style tea party or a British-inspired afternoon tea. It will be hard to "top these" at any occasion.

> **About 18 thin slices homemade-type sandwich bread, scored thin cucumber slices or scalloped thin jicima slices**
> **Paprika**
> **Fresh parsley, finely minced**
> **Green onion stems, blanched 5 seconds, chilled in iced water**
> **Whole pimento, well drained**
> **Fresh cilantro leaves**
>
> *Macadamia Chicken Spread:*
> **1 stalk fresh lemongrass or 1 teaspoon freshly grated lemon peel**
> **1 tablespoon almond or vegetable oil**
> **2 shallots, finely minced**
> **1 teaspoon finely minced fresh gingerroot**
> **3 tablespoons finely chopped macadamia nuts**
> **1/8 teaspoon ground tumeric**
> **1/2 cup Lemon-Ginger Dressing, page 130**
> **1/4 to 1/2 teaspoon ground fresh chili paste (sambal oelek) or Vietnamese-style hot chili sauce**
> **1/2 teaspoon salt**
> **Dash white pepper**
> **1 (8-oz.) chicken breast, poached, skinned, boned, finely chopped**
> **2 tablespoons coarsely chopped macadamia nuts**
> **1/4 cup Crème Fraîche, page 22, or sour cream**
> **1 tablespoon minced fresh cilantro leaves or parsley**

Prepare Macadamia Chicken Spread. If using bread, preheat broiler. With a 3-inch round cutter, cut 1 circle from each bread slice. Reserve bread crusts for another use. Place bread circles on an ungreased baking sheet; toast lightly on both sides. Place 1 tablespoon of chicken spread in center of each toast circle or vegetable slice. Smooth in rounded mounds. Sprinkle 1/2 of mounds lightly with paprika; sprinkle remainder with parsley.

Trim green onion stems and pimento in long narrow strips. Trim ends in a V-shape, if desired. Wrap a green onion strip around base of each chicken mound topped with paprika. Wrap a pimento strip around mounds topped with parsley. Cross ends to resemble ribbons on a hat. Tuck a cilantro leaf "feather" into bands. If serving chicken spread on toast rounds, serve within 30 minutes. Chicken spread served on vegetable slices can be covered and refrigerated several hours. Makes 6 servings.

Macadamia Chicken Spread:

If using lemongrass, remove tough outer stalks. Smash inner stalks, thinly slice and mince finely. In a small skillet, heat almond oil over medium heat until hot. Sauté lemongrass or lemon peel, shallots, gingerooot, finely chopped nuts and tumeric, stirring constantly, 1 to 2 minutes or until mixture softens and becomes aromatic. Remove from heat.

With a mortar and pestle or in a blender, grind mixture to a paste. Spoon into a medium-size bowl. Stir in Lemon-Ginger Dressing, chili paste, salt and white pepper. Blend chicken and coarsely chopped nuts into mixture. Stir in Crème Fraîche and cilantro. Cover and refrigerate at least 4 hours or overnight. Makes about 1-1/2 cups.

VARIATION
To prepare *Crunchy Macadamia Chicken Balls*, form chilled chicken spread in 24 balls. Roll in crushed Spicy Vermicelli Snack, page 69. Serve within 30 minutes to insure maximum crunchiness. Makes 6 servings.

Orange-Flavored Beef *China*

This is Chinese "red-cooking" or braising at its best. The spiced beef tastes best when chilled and served in thin slices. A great do-ahead appetizer! Long slow cooking in moist heat will tenderize a tougher cut of beef and permeate it with flavorful seasonings. Select a cut of beef with a great deal of connective tissue. It will yield a rich full-bodied sauce with a higher amount of natural gelatin. The richly seasoned cold jellied sauce can be chopped and served with the beef or saved and used as a seasoning for hearty stir-fry or noodle dishes.

> **2 tablespoons vegetable oil**
> **1 (2-1/2- to 3-lb.) blade-cut beef chuck roast**
> **1/2 cup fresh cilantro leaves**
>
> *Orange-Flavored Master Sauce:*
> **1-1/2 cups fresh orange juice**
> **3/4 cup medium Japanese soy sauce**
> **1/2 cup lightly packed dark-brown sugar**
> **2 whole star anise**
> **2 (1/8-inch-thick) slices fresh gingerroot, smashed**
> **1 teaspoon freshly grated orange peel**
> **1 green onion, cut in half**
> **1/4 cup dry white wine**

Prepare Orange-Flavored Master Sauce. Heat a wok or medium-size saucepan over medium-high heat 1 minute. Add oil. When oil is hot, add beef; sauté on all sides. Add Orange-Flavored Master Sauce. Bring to a boil. Reduce heat to medium-low. Cover pan and simmer beef 1-1/2 hours or until tender. Cool beef in sauce. Remove and discard star anise, gingerroot and green onion. Cut beef in paper-thin slices. Arrange slices overlapping on a serving platter. Garnish with cilantro. Reheat sauce and serve with beef, if desired. Makes 12 to 14 servings.

Orange-Flavored Master Sauce:
In a medium-size bowl, combine all ingredients. Stir to dissolve sugar. Makes about 2-1/2 cups.

VARIATION
Substitute 2 to 3 beef shanks or 3 pounds beef chuck short ribs or pork shoulder for beef chuck roast.

Spicy Onion Fritters

India

"Pakoras" (chick-pea fritters) are popular snacks throughout India. They also make a satisfying addition to a vegetarian meal. Create tasty flavors by adding other ingredients such as shredded fresh mint, shredded unsweetened coconut or chopped cashew nuts. In India "pakoras" are sometimes mixed into a bowl of creamy fresh yogurt for an unusual, but refreshing, salad-type dish. Serve with fresh Jade-Mint Raita, page 130.

1 cup chick-pea flour (besan)
1/2 teaspoon salt
1/4 teaspoon baking soda
1/2 cup water
2 tablespoons plain yogurt
2 tablespoons vegetable oil
1/2 teaspoon ground tumeric
1/2 teaspoon cumin seeds
1/2 teaspoon finely minced fresh gingerroot
1 medium-size onion, quartered, thinly sliced
1 to 2 tablespoons fresh cilantro leaves, minced
1 small fresh whole green chili pepper, stemmed, seeded, minced
4 cups peanut or vegetable oil for deep-frying

In a medium-size bowl, combine flour, salt and baking soda. In a small bowl, combine water and yogurt. Stir liquid into dry ingredients until batter is smooth and free from lumps. In a small skillet, heat 2 tablespoons oil over medium heat until hot. Add tumeric and cumin seeds. Fry 30 seconds, stirring constantly to prevent burning. When cumin seeds smell aromatic, remove pan from heat. Cool 2 to 3 minutes. Stir warm oil into batter, then stir in gingerroot, onion, cilantro and chili pepper. Cover batter and let stand 30 minutes.

In a wok or shallow saucepan, heat 4 cups oil to 360F (180C) or until a 1-inch cube of bread turns golden-brown in 60 seconds. Using 1 generous tablespoon of batter per fritter, drop 4 to 5 fritters into hot oil. Fry slowly 5 or 6 minutes, turning several times to insure complete doneness. Fritters should be dark golden-brown and have a delicate crispy coating when done. Drain on paper towels. Repeat with remaining batter. Serve within 30 minutes to enjoy crispy texture. Makes 4 to 5 servings.

HINT
Batter can be covered and refrigerated several hours. Bring back to room temperature before frying. Fritters can be fried until light golden-brown 3 to 4 hours before serving. To serve, fry again in hot oil 375F (190C) 45 seconds to 1 minute or until dark golden-brown. Or reheat in a preheated oven 350F (175C) 8 to 10 minutes.

Shredded Beef & Almonds in Lettuce Cups, pages 36-37

Curried Lamb Crescents with Pine Nuts & Apricot Sauce

North China

Thirteenth-century Mongolians of China's Yuan dynasty enjoyed a diet far different from the one eaten throughout China today. Strong European influences brought about the regular use of milk, butter and lamb. A cookbook written by an official of that period informs us that dumplings were filled with lamb and flavored with orange peel. Foods were seasoned with pine nuts, rose water and almond oil. Jams were made from sugar and fruits such as peaches, lemons and quince. Fried lamb crescents offer us a taste of the spirit and flavor of the Mongolian cuisine. To prepare baked crescents, substitute one recipe Basic Tender Butter Pastry, page 27, or two recipes Golden Flaky Pastry, page 28. Roll pastry one-eighth-inch thick; cut in three-inch circles. Bake the crescents at 375F (190C) until golden-brown. (Photo of *Apricot Sauce* on cover.)

1 (10-oz.) package round Japanese gyoza skins or 1 pound
    square Chinese won ton skins cut in 3-inch circles
1 egg, slightly beaten
6 cups peanut or vegetable oil for deep-frying

Apricot Sauce:
1 cup sugar
1/2 teaspon salt
1/3 cup ketchup
1/2 cup rice vinegar
1 cup apricot preserves
Freshly grated peel 1 lemon
1 tablespoon lemon juice
3 tablespoons cornstarch
1 cup unsweetened pineapple juice
1 teaspoon ground fresh chili paste (sambal oelek), if desired

Curried Lamb Filling:
2 tablespoons vegetable oil
1 small onion, finely chopped
1 generous teaspoon finely minced gingerroot
2 large garlic cloves, finely minced
12 ounces lean ground lamb
1 tablespoon curry powder
1 teaspoon freshly grated orange peel
3 tablespoons dry white wine
2 tablespoons soy sauce
1 scant teaspoon cornstarch
1/3 cup chicken stock
1/4 cup lightly toasted pine nuts
Salt to taste

Prepare Apricot Sauce and Curried Lamb Filling. Place 1 generous teaspoon of filling in center of each skin. Fold skins in half, forming crescents. Seal edges with beaten egg, pressing sealed edges tightly to prevent opening during frying. Cover formed dumplings with plastic wrap. In a wok or shallow heavy saucepan, heat oil to 360F (175C) or until a 1-inch cube of bread turns brown in 60 seconds. Fry several crescents at a time 2 to 3 minutes or until filling is cooked and pastry is crisp and golden-brown. Turn several times to insure even-browning. Drain on paper towels. Serve with Apricot Sauce. Makes about 60 dumplings.

Apricot Sauce:
In a medium-size saucepan, combine sugar, salt, ketchup, rice vinegar, apricot preserves and lemon peel and juice. Place over medium heat. In a small bowl, dissolve cornstarch in pineapple juice. Stir into preserve mixture. Cook and stir until mixture has come to a boil and thickened. Stir in chili paste, if desired. Makes about 3 cups.

Curried Lamb Filling:
In a wok or large skillet, heat oil over medium heat until hot. Add onion, gingerroot and garlic; stir-fry 2 to 3 minutes or until soft. Add lamb; stir-fry 1 to 2 minutes. Stir in curry powder. Continue cooking until lamb is crumbly and no longer pink. Stir in orange peel, wine and soy sauce. In a small bowl, combine cornstarch and chicken stock. Stir into lamb and cook until mixture is slightly glazed. Stir in nuts and salt. Makes about 2-1/4 cups.

HINT
Uncooked crescents can be wrapped well and frozen 2 to 3 weeks. Thaw before cooking.

Crispy Potato Patties with Cashew Nuts
India

These crunchy golden potato patties are almost as light as beignets. Mashed potatoes are blended with Golden Egg-Puff Paste, page 29, spices and cashew nuts, then formed in patties and deep-fried. Serve potato patties with your favorite chutney or relish as an unusual and delicious appetizer or snack or as a vegetable side dish.

> **4 medium-size baking potatoes, scrubbed, pricked with a fork**
> **1 cup Golden Egg-Puff Paste, page 29**
> **1/4 cup plain yogurt**
> **2 tablespoons vegetable oil**
> **1/2 cup finely chopped onion**
> **1/2 teaspoon cumin seeds**
> **1/2 teaspoon salt**
> **1/8 teaspoon freshly grated nutmeg**
> **1/4 cup finely chopped roasted cashew nuts**
> **4 cups peanut or vegetable oil for deep-frying**
> **All-purpose flour**

Preheat oven to 425F (220C). Bake potatoes on middle rack of preheated oven 1 hour or until tender when pressed. Cool 10 minutes. Remove pulp and mash with a potato masher; measure 2 cups. Reserve leftover potatoes for another use. In a medium-size bowl, combine potatoes, Golden Egg-Puff Paste and yogurt. In a small skillet, heat 2 tablespoons oil over medium heat until hot. Stir in onion and cumin seeds; cook 1 minute. Cool slightly; stir into potato mixture. Add salt, nutmeg and nuts. Blend well.

In a wok or heavy shallow saucepan, heat 4 cups oil to 360F (180C) or until a 1-inch cube of bread turns golden-brown in 60 seconds. Lightly oil a tablespoon. Form 1 generous tablespoon of potato mixture in a pattie about 2-inches wide. Repeat with remaining potato mixture. Coat patties lightly with flour. Fry 5 or 6 patties at a time, 4 to 5 minutes or until crust is crispy and medium golden-brown. Drain on paper towels. Serve hot or at room temperature. Patties retain their delicate crispiness about 2 hours. Makes 6 to 8 servings.

To serve **Lemon-Chicken Pâté with Fresh Basil**, *slice the delicate lemon-flavored chicken pâté and enclose in flaky buttery croissants. Tuck colorful green bibb lettuce leaves inside for a tempting and stunning presentation.*

Sake-Glazed Mushrooms *Japan*

Use these rich-tasting simmered dried forest mushrooms to add flavor to rice and noodle dishes or meat mixtures. Cut the mushrooms in small pieces and serve as a snack.

> **4 medium-size to large dried shiitake mushrooms**
> **1 cup water**
>
> *Glazing Sauce:*
> **1 cup water**
> **1/2 teaspoon instant Japanese soup stock (dashi-no-moto)**
> **2 tablespoons soy sauce**
> **2 tablespoons sugar**
> **2 tablespoons Japanese sweet rice wine (mirin)**
> **2 tablespoons sake**

In a medium-size bowl, cover mushrooms with water; soak 30 minutes. Prepare Glazing Sauce. In a small saucepan, combine mushrooms and Glazing Sauce. Cook over high heat. When liquid boils, reduce heat to medium-low. Simmer 20 to 25 minutes or until mushrooms are well seasoned and liquid is almost completely reduced. Cool mushrooms. Cut off and discard stems. Cut mushrooms in strips or mince. Recipe can be doubled. Makes 4 seasoned mushrooms.

Glazing Sauce:
In a small bowl, combine all ingredients.

Lemon-Chicken Pâté
with Fresh Basil

Viet Nam

The inspiration behind this Vietnamese-style chicken pâté is Ai Ba Li, owner of a successful French-Vietnamese pastry shop-restaurant complex in Virginia. Famous for his charcuterie, Mr. Li introduced me to the technique of making this delicate chicken pâté which is similar in texture and appearance to the French "boudin blanc." Chicken forcemeat is delicately seasoned with lemongrass and fresh basil, then steamed in sausage-shaped rolls. Serve it with Bibb lettuce leaves on buttery croissants. It is also delicious served on a bed of lettuce with Nuoc Cham Dipping Sauce, page 136, as an elegant appetizer.

1 stalk fresh lemongrass or 1 teaspoon freshly grated lemon peel
2 tablespoons vegetable oil
4 green onions, thinly sliced
1 pound skinned boned chicken breast halves, cut in pieces
2 teaspoons salt
1/4 teaspoon white pepper
1/2 teaspoon freshly grated nutmeg
1 teaspoon Southeast Asian fish sauce (nuoc mam)
1 tablespoon rice flour
2 large egg whites
3/4 cup whipping cream
1 tablespoon finely minced fresh basil
1 teaspoon ground fresh chili paste (sambal oelek), if desired

If using lemongrass, remove tough outer stalks. Smash inner stalks, thinly slice and mince finely. In a small skillet, heat oil over medium-low heat. Cook lemongrass or lemon peel and green onions 45 seconds or just until aromatic. Remove from heat; cool slightly. Slice chicken in strips. In a blender or food processor fitted with the steel blade, process green onion mixture with oil and chicken to a paste consistency. Blend in salt, white pepper, nutmeg, fish sauce and rice flour. Blend egg whites quickly into mixture. Remove mixture to a large bowl.

With an electric mixer, beat whipping cream in a small chilled bowl about 1 minute or only until slightly thickened; it should not form soft peaks. Blend thickened cream into chicken mixture in 2 to 3 portions. Mix in fresh basil and chili paste, if desired; divide in half. On a large piece of plastic wrap, pat and shape 1/2 of chicken mixture in a 6- to 7-inch-long sausage-shaped roll. With oiled hands, wrap roll in plastic wrap, continuing to pat chicken mixture in a sausage-shape. Repeat with remaining chicken mixture. Refrigerate 2 to 3 hours.

In a wok or deep pot, bring 4 cups water to a boil. Place chicken rolls in a small shallow baking pan. Place pan on a steamer tray; cover tray. Place over boiling water. Steam 10 to 12 minutes or just until chicken turns white and becomes firm to touch. Remove chicken rolls from pan. Cool to room temperature. Remove plastic wrap. Wrap pâté in fresh plastic wrap. Refrigerate 2 to 3 days for best flavor. Slice to desired thickeness. Makes 10 to 12 servings.

HINT
Pâté can be stored in refrigerator up to 1 week.

Chili Beef Puffs with Peanuts & Fresh Basil

Thailand

The idea for these spicy little meat puffs came about after I had the opportunity to observe Thai cooks experiment with classic cream-puff paste. They meticulously made delicious, savory pastries by layering French cream puff paste with spicy meat curry. To speed things up, I mixed the paste and a meat curry together, then dropped small mounds of the mixture into miniature muffin tins for baking. To cool things down, I reduced the original amount of chilies by half! Depending on your time and your heat tolerance, try them either way. For a "dynamite" rice dish, mix three cups cold cooked rice into a skillet of spicy Chili-Beef.

2 tablespoons minced fresh basil
2 tablespoons chopped roasted peanuts
1 green onion, minced
1 recipe Golden Egg-Puff Paste, page 29

Chili-Beef:
2 stalks fresh lemongrass or 2 teaspoons freshly grated lemon peel
1/4 teaspoon ground cloves
1/2 teaspoon ground cardamon
1 teaspoon cumin seeds
1/4 teaspoon freshly grated nutmeg
3/4 teaspoon salt
1/8 teaspoon black pepper
2 tablespoons vegetable oil
2 shallots, finely minced
4 large garlic cloves, finely minced
1 teaspoon finely minced fresh gingerroot
2 to 3 small dried whole red chili peppers, stemmed, seeded, minced
1/2 pound lean ground beef

Preheat oven to 400F (205C). Prepare Chili-Beef. Stir Chili-Beef, basil, peanuts and green onion into Golden Egg-Puff Paste. Using 1 tablespoonful of mixture per puff, fill 3 nonstick miniature muffin pans. Bake in preheated oven on middle rack 18 to 20 minutes or until puffy and golden-brown. Do not underbake or puffs might collapse. Cool 2 to 3 minutes. Remove from pans. Serve warm or at room temperature. Makes about 36 puffs.

Chili Beef:
If using lemongrass, remove tough outer stalks. Smash inner stalks, thinly slice and mince finely. In a small bowl, mix cloves, cardamon, cumin seeds, nutmeg, salt and black pepper. In a wok or medium-size skillet, heat oil over medium-high heat until hot. Add lemongrass or lemon peel, shallots, garlic and gingerroot. Stir-fry 1 minute. Watch carefully to prevent burning. Add spice mixture. Stir-fry 1 minute or until mixture becomes fragrant. Stir in chili peppers. Add beef; cook until no longer pink and well blended with spice mixture. Break up any large pieces. Drain off any fat. Remove mixture to a platter to cool. Makes about 1 cup.

HINT
Puffs can be prepared ahead and frozen. Thaw and reheat in a preheated oven 375F (190C) 8 to 10 minutes or until hot.

STARTERS

The types of salads and soups consummed in Asia vary widely geographically. They are made from combinations of fresh ingredients such as vegetables, beans, seafood, noodles, yogurt, poultry and even beef.

Salads as we know them do not exist in China. Raw vegetables are unsafe to be eaten in large amounts. Instead they are usually lightly steamed, stir-fried or blanched. Chinese cold-mixed foods closely embraces our concept of salad. Quickly cooked foods, such as mung bean noodles and shredded vegetables, are tossed together with a tangy vinegar and soy sauce dressing and served at room temperature.

Salads in Japan are also served as appetizers. Unlike other Asian countries, salads are eaten on a regular basis in Japan. They are classified under the names of "Sunomono" and "Aemono." In "Sunomono," the ingredients are mixed with a thin, tangy dressing. Salads which are considered "Aemono" are made up of mixed ingredients coated with a mild-tasting, slightly thickened dressing. Shrimp & Kiwifruit in Lemon-Kimizu Dressing, page 66, is considered an "Aemono." Both types of salads are served in small portions and are selected to complement the other dishes in taste, texture and color.

Soups are a simple and basic food capable of serving many needs. At a formal dinner in China, soup might be served once or twice throughout the various courses of a meal; the final soup serving would come during the last course. During a regular meal at home or in a restaurant, a bowl of light soup with a few added ingredients is served along with individual bowls of rice, meat and vegetable side dishes. The soup serves as a beverage which is for sipping during the meal and helps clear the palate for new tastes yet to come.

This curious custom is actually based upon practicality. The water in China is generally unsanitary and unfit to drink without boiling. Boiled soup is a safe method of consumming water during meals. Many Chinese people like to mix some of their soup right into their rice bowls as they are eating their soup. This type of light soup is based upon the use of a good chicken stock such as Gingery Chicken Stock, page 26. Small bowls of soup served at the beginning of a Chinese meal is strictly a western-style custom, and certainly, a custom which suits our needs. Heavier, more substantial soups should be served as main dishes. If you wish, fortify them with servings of steamed or baked Chinese buns or servings of fried dumplings.

Royal Indian Almond Soup with Saffron   *India*

Perfumed with saffron, this exquisite, golden-hued cream soup is elegant enough to grace the table of a grand Moghul emperor. Spicing has been kept to a minimum to allow the gentle essence of saffron and delicate flavor of the almonds to shine through. Prized since antiquity, saffron threads are the dried stigmas of the blue or purple crocus. Saffron is the world's most precious and costly spice. Crush the threads; soak in a small amount of liquid to release the flavor oils and rich golden color. In India, saffron and almonds are regarded as very special ingredients for cooking and garniture. You will think this soup is special too!

1 cup whipping cream
1/4 teaspoon crushed saffron threads
2 tablespoons Ghee, page 25, or unsalted butter
3 shallots, thinly sliced
1 cup blanched slivered almonds
3 cups Gingery Chicken Stock, page 26, more if needed
2 tablespoons cornstarch
1/2 teaspoon salt
Dash white pepper

Embellishments:
1/2 poached chicken breast, skinned, boned, cut in small cubes
1/4 cup toasted sliced almonds
1/4 cup Crispy Fried Shallots, page 26
Spicy Vermicelli Snack, page 69, as desired
2 small green onions, finely minced

In a small bowl, combine 1/2 cup of whipping cream and saffron. In a medium-size saucepan, melt Ghee over medium heat. Add shallots and almonds. Cook, stirring constantly, until almonds are golden-brown. Remove from heat. In a blender or food processor fitted with the steel blade, process almond mixture until almost a paste consistency. Spoon mixture back into saucepan. Blend in Gingery Chicken Stock. Cover tightly and simmer over low heat 20 minutes.

Strain and press hot mixture through a fine mesh strainer into a medium-size bowl. Discard almond pulp. Measure 2-1/2 cups. If mixture does not measure 2-1/2 cups, add additional stock. Rinse saucepan. Reserve 1/2 cup of almond-stock mixture; return remainder to saucepan. Cook over medium-high heat until mixture comes to a boil. Stir cornstarch into reserved almond-stock mixture; stir into soup mixture. Cook, stirring constantly, 1 minute or until soup thickens. Reduce heat. Stir in whipping cream and saffron, salt and white pepper. Reduce heat; simmer gently 2 to 3 minutes. Serve hot with Embellishments. Makes 4 to 5 servings.

Embellishments:
Select at least 2 to 3 Embellishments. Pass separately in small serving dishes.

Creamy Asparagus Soup with Crabmeat *Viet Nam*

The Vietnamese use of asparagus, butter and cream reflect the French influence from almost a century of Colonial rule. When you taste this delicate soup you will experience a wide range of subtle flavors which blend together in perfect harmony. The tiny lime buds add a refreshing and altogether unexpected flavor surprise!

1 (10-oz.) package frozen asparagus spears, thawed
1 tablespoon vegetable oil, more if needed
2 shallots, thinly sliced
1 quart Gingery Chicken Stock, page 26
1-1/2 teaspoons salt
1/8 teaspoon white pepper
1 teaspoon sugar
1-1/2 tablespoons cornstarch
3 tablespoons water or chicken stock
2 tablespoons whipping cream, more if desired
1 tablespoon unsalted butter
1/2 teaspoon Southeast Asian fish sauce (nuoc mam)
6 ounces fresh lump crabmeat or frozen lump crabmeat, thawed
1 green onion, minced
10 to 12 fresh cilantro leaves, shredded
6 to 8 fresh mint leaves
1 medium-size lime, thinly sliced

Gently press excess liquid from asparagus with paper towels. Cut 2-inch tips from 4 stalks of asparagus. Slice tips diagonally and reserve. Cut each remaining stalk in 3 pieces. In a medium-size saucepan, heat oil over medium-high heat until hot. Add shallots; sauté until tender. Add asparagus pieces. Cook, stirring constantly, 1 minute. In a blender or food processor fitted with the steel blade, puree shallots and asparagus. If necessary, add up to 1/2 cup of Gingery Chicken Stock for easier blending. Pour puree into pan. Blend in remaining stock, salt, white pepper and sugar.

In a small bowl, combine cornstarch and water until smooth. Bring soup to a boil; stir in cornstarch mixture. Cook, stirring constantly, 1 minute or until slightly thickened. Reduce heat to low. Stir in whipping cream, butter, fish sauce, crabmeat, green onion, cilantro and mint, then stir in reserved asparagus tips. Reserve 6 lime slices. Cut rind from remaining slices. Carefully remove 1 tablespoon unbroken tiny lime buds; stir into soup. Garnish each bowl of soup with a reserved lime slice. Makes 6 servings.

VARIATION
Substitute 1 pound fresh asparagus for frozen asparagus. Snap off woody ends. Peel outer stalks; cut stalks in small pieces. Sauté with shallots 2 to 3 minutes. Add 1 additional cup Gingery Chicken Stock to soup mixture; simmer 10 to 12 minutes or until asparagus is tender. Proceed with recipe as instructed.

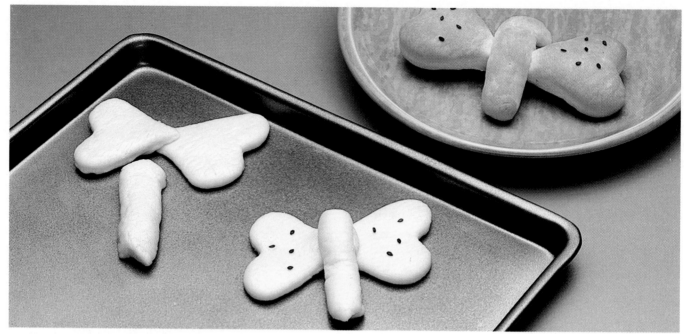

To form **Celestial Bread Dough-Butterflies**, *cut out hearts of dough and place pairs of hearts on a baking sheet with tips touching. Firmly press moistened oblong-shaped "bodies" onto middles of the joined hearts. Sprinkle with black sesame seeds, if desired, and bake until golden-brown.*

Celestial Bread-Dough Butterflies   *Chinese*

Chinese painters and poets have portrayed the butterfly as a romantic symbol, a Chinese cupid. The butterfly has been immortalized in Chinese paintings, embroidery, verse and song. When you nibble upon golden butterfly wings, think of summertime, happiness and love!

> **1 recipe Basic Chinese Yeast Bread, Chinese-Style Steamed Sandwich**
>   **Buns, page 116**
> **Water**
> **1 large egg, beaten**
> **1 teaspoon water**
> **Black Dry Roasted Sesame Seeds or poppy seeds, if desired**

Preheat oven to 350F (175C). Cut dough in half. On a lightly floured surface, roll out 1/2 of dough at a time 1/4-inch thick. Keep remaining dough covered. With a 2-inch heart-shaped cutter, cut out a pair of hearts for each set of butterfly wings. On a baking sheet, place 2 hearts with ends running horizontally with tips or bottoms of hearts touching. Leave space between butterflies so dough can rise and slightly spread.

To form bodies, tear off small pieces of dough; roll in oblong shapes, rounded and larger at top and tapered at other end. Lightly moisten portion of larger parts with water, then firmly press pieces onto middle of joined hearts. In a small bowl, beat egg with 1 teaspoon water; brush butterflies. Sprinkle black Dry Roasted Sesame Seeds on wings, if desired. Bake in preheated oven 12 to 15 minutes or until light golden-brown. Cool completely. Store in an airtight container. Makes about 24 butterflies.

Mandarin Orange Fruit Soup

China

Bursting with flavor, this hot, tangy fruit soup can be served as a dessert soup with The Ultimate Chinese Almond Cookie, page 154, or as a palate cleanser between courses in a multicourse Asian meal. Many times I have served it for breakfast or brunch in small porcelain Chinese teacups. The secret to the success of the soup is simple: use freshly squeezed, slightly tart orange juice with full flavor. Navel or Valencia oranges provide excellent quality juice.

> **1/4 cup plus 1 tablespoon sugar**
> **3 tablespoons cornstarch**
> **2 cups spring water or tap water**
> **2 cups freshly squeezed orange juice**
> **2 drops vanilla extract**
> **Pinch salt**
> **1 mandarin orange, tangerine or orange, peeled, segmented, chopped in small pieces**
> **1/4 cup mandarin orange liqueur or orange-flavored liqueur to taste, if desired**

In a medium-size saucepan, combine sugar and cornstarch. Stir in water until smooth. Bring to a boil over medium-high heat. Cook, stirring constantly, 30 seconds or until thickened. Blend in orange juice, vanilla, salt and mandarin orange. Reduce heat to medium; heat until hot. Do not allow soup to boil. Stir in mandarin orange liqueur, if desired. Serve hot. Makes 4 to 5 servings.

VARIATION
Substitute 1 (11-oz.) can mandarin orange segments, drained and chopped, for fresh orange.

HINT
Soup can be prepared 1 hour ahead. Reheat gently over low heat.

Imitate the Chinese and enhance the flavor of your favorite green tea, Oolong tea or black tea by adding delightful scents such as whole dried cloves, cinnamon sticks, dried orange blossoms or rose petals, dried lemon verbena or dried mint, strips of dried lemon or orange peel or vanilla pods. Select one or combine two or three to create your own special brand of scented tea, a great gift-giving idea.

Indonesian Chicken Soup

Indonesia

This enticing soup-stew is popular throughout Indonesia and Malaysia. Your family and guests can "build" their own bowl of soup by adding their choice of hearty accompaniments before ladeling in the soup. East Indians love to eat this dish with lots of small fiery chilies. Somehow, I savor the flavor best when I can taste the peppery bite of the chili paste. Stir two or three Side Dishes into the basic soup to be served as a first course. Accompany the soup with the entire selection of Side Dishes for a hearty main-dish soup. Prepare soup and Side Dishes one day ahead for a minimum of last minute fuss.

1 stalk fresh lemongrass or 1 teaspoon freshly grated lemon peel
2 large garlic cloves, finely minced
4 large shallots, finely minced
1 tablespoon grated fresh gingerroot
2 tablespoons vegetable oil
1/2 teaspoon ground tumeric
1 teaspoon whole black peppercorns
2-1/2 quarts Gingery Chicken Stock, page 26, reserve cooked chicken
Salt to taste

Side Dishes:
2 ounces dried rice-stick noodles
1/2 pound fresh bean sprouts
Reserved cooked chicken, shredded
1 recipe Pressed Rice Cakes, page 73 or Pressed Coconut Rice Cakes, page 73
1 recipe Tofu Nuggets, Crispy Fried Tofu Nuggets with Condiments, page 68
4 hard-cooked eggs, cut in slices or wedges
1 recipe Crispy Fried Shallots, page 26
Ground fresh chili paste (sambal oelek) to taste
1/2 cup fresh celery leaves
6 green onions, thinly sliced
4 limes, cut in wedges
1/2 cup fresh cilantro leaves

Prepare Side Dishes. If using lemongrass, remove tough outer stalks. Smash inner stalks, thinly slice and mince finely. With a mortar and pestle, crush lemongrass or lemon peel, garlic, shallots and gingerroot to a paste. Or use a large knife to finely mince ingredients. In a large pot, heat oil over medium heat until hot. Add paste; stir until fragrant, about 30 seconds. Add tumeric and peppercorns; stir 1 minute more.

   Remove pot from heat. Pour in most of stock. Use remaining stock to rinse any seasonings from mortar; pour into pot. Bring stock to a boil. Reduce heat. Simmer, partially covered, 5 minutes. Add salt. Strain stock to remove peppercorns, if desired. Invite guests to place desired Side Dishes into deep soup bowls. Ladle hot soup into each filled bowl. Makes 6 to 8 servings.

Side Dishes:

In a medium-size bowl, cover rice noodles with cool water; soak at least 15 minutes. In a medium-size saucepan, simmer 1 quart water and rice noodles over medium heat 1 to 2 minutes. Drain rice noodles. Pour boiling water over bean sprouts in a colander. Immediately plunge sprouts into iced water; when chilled, drain well. Spread on a kitchen towel or paper towels to absorb excess moisture. Pat gently until dry. Arrange Side Dishes in individual serving dishes.

VARIATION
Add 1 (2-inch) stick cinnamon and 1/2 (4 points) whole star anise to fried spice paste with tumeric and peppercorns. Strain soup to remove all spices.

To serve **Kyoko's Rainbow in Spring Rain**, *arrange prismatic rainbow shreds of ham, vegetables and egg in a cartwheel pattern over a layer of transparent been thread noodles for a colorful presentation.*

When cooking rice, always consider the moisture content because it will vary with the type and age of rice, humidity and method of cooking. Older rice will need more water than new rice. Make adjustments in the water amounts, as desired. Opinions vary greatly on the merits of rinsing rice before cooking. In Southeast Asia, rice is always carefully rinsed before cooking to remove talc coatings or foreign matter. The rice is less starchy after cooking and has a sweet, fresh odor and taste. Rinsing rice for making sushi helps it to absorb the dressing better.

Cook rice in a solid flat-bottomed pan of the proper size. Be sure it has a tight-fitting lid. An automatic electric rice cooker is an excellent investment. It cooks perfect rice every time and frees oven burners for other jobs. Always follow the manufacturer's directions for usage. Never add hot water to rice in the rice cooker; use cool tap water instead. Hot water will "confuse" the sensitive electric thermostat into believing the rice is already partially done. Instead of soft, plump rice, you will end up with hard, dry grains.

Kyoko's Rainbow in Spring Rain   *Japan*

This simple noodle dish is low in calories and beautiful to behold. I prepared it for sophisticated foodies during cooking classes at Sakonnette Vineyards in Rhode Island; it was an instant hit! A layer of "harusame" (soaked transparent Japanese bean thread noodles) is spread over the serving platter. A rainbow of vegetable, egg and ham shreds are placed decoratively over the top. Each guest helps himself to a portion of the noodles and toppings, then drizzles on a light, tangy sauce. At the table, everyone tosses his own individual portion. Translated, "harusame" means spring rain. In the poetic sense as well as literally, guests are sure to enjoy the colorful sight of the prismatic rainbow shreds glistening in "spring rain"!

4 ounces thin Japanese bean thread noodles (harusame) or Taiwanese bean threads
1 bunch radish sprouts (kaiwari daikon), fresh cilantro leaves or watercress

Tangy Sesame Sauce:
1 cup rice vinegar
1 tablespoon plus 1 teaspoon medium Japanese soy sauce
1/4 cup plus 2 tablespoons sugar
2 teaspoons sesame seed oil
1/2 teaspoon salt
1 teaspoon Dry Roasted Sesame Seeds, page 24

Rainbow Shreds:
3 to 4 (1-oz.) thin slices baked ham, shredded
1 large carrot, thinly sliced diagonally, shredded
2 ounces fresh Chinese pea pods, blanched 30 seconds, chilled in iced water, shredded
1 medium-size red bell pepper, ends trimmed, seeded, ribs removed, shredded
1 recipe Egg Crepe, page 24, shredded
6 green onions, smashed, shredded

In a large bowl, cover noodles with water which has been brought to a boil; soak 30 minutes. If using skeins of Taiwanese bean threads, soak with bindings in place. Cut in shorter lengths after soaking; remove bindings. Prepare Tangy Sesame Sauce. Drain noodles. On a round serving platter, spread noodles. Arrange Rainbow Shreds on top to resemble spokes of a wheel. Place a cluster of radish sprouts in center of toppings. Serve with Tangy Sesame Sauce. Makes 6 to 8 servings.

Tangy Sesame Sauce:
In a medium-size bowl, combine all ingredients. Stir until sugar dissolves. Use immediately or cover and refrigerate until serving time. Makes about 1-1/4 cups.

HINT
All Rainbow Shreds, except green onions, can be prepared and refrigerated in separate covered containers until needed.

Korean Bulgogi Salad

Korea

Korean celebrations center around the home; food and its preparation are the unifying thread. A family's reputation might depend on the amount and quality of the foods prepared. Noodles are a symbol of longevity served during special occasions with hope they will bring long life and good luck. Fresh vegetables and garden greens play an important part in the Korean diet. Wild mountain and field plants such as fiddlehead ferns, shepard's purse and mugwart are highly regarded. The addition of any of these would be delightful. The bean-paste dressing makes an exceptionally delicious sauce for steamed vegetables or grilled steak.

1/2 pound bean sprouts
12 ounces dried Korean-style buckwheat noodles (naeng myun) or Chinese egg
   noodles, cooked al dente, rinsed in cold water, drained well
1 tablespoon sesame seed or vegetable oil
Seven-spice mixture (shichimi togarashi) to taste
1 recipe Sake-Glazed Mushrooms, page 46, shredded
1 recipe Egg Crepe, page 24, shredded
1 small red bell pepper, ends trimmed, seeded, ribs removed, cut in matchstick
   julienne strips
1 recipe Korean-Style Grilled Spicy Beef, page 121
1 bunch loose-leaf spinach leaves
3 green onions, thinly sliced
1/3 cup toasted pine nuts

Red Pepper Paste Dressing:
2 large garlic cloves
2 (1/8-inch-thick) slices fresh gingerroot
1/4 cup plus 2 tablespoons red wine vinegar
2 tablespoons medium Japanese soy sauce
2 teaspoons sesame seed oil
2 tablespoons brown sugar
2 generous tablespoons Korean bean paste (kochu jang)
1 teaspoon salt
Several dashes black pepper
2 cups vegetable oil
2 tablespoons Dry Roasted Sesame Seeds, page 24

Prepare Red Pepper Paste Dressing. Pour boiling water over bean sprouts in a colander. Immediately plunge sprouts into iced water; when chilled, drain well. Spread on a kitchen towel or paper towels to absorb excess moisture. Pat gently until dry. Coat noodles with sesame seed oil. Sprinkle with seven-spice mixture. In a large bowl, combine bean sprouts, noodles, Sake-Glazed Mushrooms, Egg Crepe and bell pepper. Cover and refrigerate until needed. Tear each slice of Korean Style Grilled Spicy Beef in 2 or 3 pieces. Stir any juices from beef into dressing, if desired.

    Cover a large round platter with spinach leaves. Spoon noodle mixture in a thin layer over spinach leaves. Mound beef in middle of noodle mixture; sprinkle with green onions and nuts. Serve with Red Pepper Paste Dressing. Makes 6 to 8 servings.

Red Pepper Paste Dressing:
With motor running of a blender or food processor fitted with the steel blade, drop in garlic and gingerroot. Process until finely chopped. Stop machine. Add vinegar, soy sauce, sesame seed oil, brown sugar, bean paste, salt and black pepper. With machine running, pour in vegetable oil. Process just until all vegetable oil has been added and dressing is slightly thickened. Stir in Dry Roasted Sesame Seeds. Cover and refrigerate until needed. Makes 2 cups.

Farida's Fried Eggplant in Spiced Yogurt Sauce

West Pakistan

Throughout history, foods have been combined and seasoned in a variety of ways to form light, refreshing salads. In Pakistan and India, tangy yogurt is blended with an endless combination of vegetables, herbs and spices to form yogurt-based dishes called "raitas." Farida Naqvi of Karachi, Pakistan shared this delicious, do-ahead recipe which combines a spicy yogurt "raita" with fried eggplant, a vegetable native to India. The eggplant can be finely chopped and stirred into the spiced yogurt for a tasty dip with wedges of fresh pita bread. Or serve the spiced yogurt mixture alone as a refreshing side dish. Crème Fraîche, page 22, or sour cream improves the consistency and flavor of our domestic yogurt. This is best served within 48 hours. Recipe can be doubled.

> **2 (1- to 1-1/4 lb.) eggplants, unpeeled**
> **Salt to taste**
> **Vegetable oil for frying**
> **1/4 cup chopped fresh cilantro or parsley leaves**
>
> *Spiced Yogurt with Cucumber & Tomato:*
> **1 (8-oz.) carton plain yogurt**
> **2 heaping tablespoons Crème Fraîche, page 22, or sour cream**
> **1/2 cup peeled seeded finely chopped cucumber**
> **1/2 cup seeded finely chopped tomato**
> **1/4 cup finely chopped onion**
> **1/2 teaspoon ground cumin**
> **1/8 teaspoon black pepper**
> **1/2 teaspoon salt**
> **1 small fresh whole green chili pepper, stemmed, seeded, minced**

Prepare Spiced Yogurt with Cucumber & Tomato. Cut eggplant in 1-inch slices; sprinkle lightly with salt. Place slices in a colander sitting over a pan. Let stand 30 minutes to allow salt to draw out any bitter juices. Pat eggplant slices dry with paper towels. In a large skillet, heat 1/2-inch oil over high heat to 370F (190C) or until a 1-inch cube of bread turns golden-brown in 50 seconds. Fry 1 layer of eggplant in hot oil 3 to 4 minutes or until light golden-brown on both sides. Drain on paper towels. Repeat with remaining slices.

Cool and cut each eggplant slice in quarter sections. In a medium-size shallow casserole dish, spread half of eggplant over bottom. Spoon 1/2 of Spiced Yogurt with Cucumber & Tomato over eggplant. Repeat with remaining eggplant and spiced yogurt. Sprinkle with cilantro. Serve at once or cover and refrigerate. Makes 4 servings.

Spiced Yogurt with Cucumber & Tomato:
In a medium-size bowl, combine all ingredients. Cover and refrigerate at least 30 minutes or up to 24 hours. Makes about 2-1/2 cups.

Luzon Shrimp & Hearts of Palm Salad with Creamy Lime Vinaigrette
Philippines

In the sixteenth century, the Spanish traveled to the Philippines and stayed for 400 years! They left behind many facets of their culture and cuisine, now firmly entrenched in the Filipino way of life. Earlier Polynesian and Malaysian ancestors also left behind a rich heritage of culinary gifts. Hearts of palm, or "palmito" in Spanish, are a favorite ingredient in many Filipino dishes. Also called swamp cabbage, the heart of palm is a cream-colored stalk resembling white asparagus and comes from the heart of the cabbage palmetto or palm tree. This elegant Filipino salad has European overtones and hints of the tropics; it seems very international indeed! Delight your friends and serve it with Spanish-Style Chicken Pies with Laurel Leaf Pastry, pages 82-83, for "merienda sienna," the late afternoon Filipino high-tea.

Fresh bibb lettuce leaves or baby bok choy leaves
1 pound fresh large shrimp, cooked, peeled, deveined
1 (16-oz.) can hearts of palm, drained, cut in 1/2-inch-thick slices
1 green or ripe mango, peeled, seeded, sliced
1 small red Bermuda onion, thinly sliced
1/3 cup whole pitted black olives
2 tablespoons julienne strips pimento
6 hard-cooked quail eggs or 3 small hard-cooked eggs, cut in half

Creamy Lime Vinaigrette:
1 large garlic clove
1 (1/8-inch-thick) slice fresh gingerroot
2 medium-size green onions with stems, cut in 1-inch lengths
1 teaspoon freshly grated lime peel
1/4 cup fresh lime juice
1/4 cup white cider or rice vinegar
1/4 cup sugar
1 teaspoon salt
Several dashes white pepper
1/2 teaspoon sesame seed oil
1-1/2 cups almond or vegetable oil
1/3 cup Light Coconut Milk, page 21, or slightly diluted canned coconut milk
Thin strips lime peel

Prepare Creamy Lime Vinaigrette. Arrange ingredients on a serving platter or individual serving plates. Serve with Creamy Lime Vinaigrette. Makes 6 servings.

Creamy Lime Vinaigrette:
With motor running of a blender or food processor fitted with the steel blade, drop in garlic, gingerroot and green onions. Process until finely chopped. Stop machine. Add grated lime peel, lime juice, vinegar, sugar, salt, white pepper and sesame seed oil. Process until smooth. With machine running, slowly pour in almond oil; process just until oil is blended and vinaigrette is slightly thickened. Add Light Coconut Milk; process quickly to blend. Pour dressing into a container; cover and refrigerate until chilled. Decorate with lime peel strips. Makes 1-1/2 cups.

Luzon Shrimp & Hearts of Palm Salad with Creamy Lime Vinaigrette; Spanish-Style Chicken Pies with Laurel Leaf Pastry, pages 82-83

Chicken Packets with Eight Precious Condiments

This variation on the popular Chinese chicken salad theme is easy to prepare and creates a stunning presentation for a buffet. A serving platter centered with shredded flavorful poached chicken is surrounded by a kaleidoscope of eight colorful condiments offering a full range of taste contrasts and textural crunch. The chicken tastes best served at room temperature, shredded just before serving. If refrigerated, bring to room temperature before serving. The chicken and condiments are encased in crisp lettuce leaves and sprinkled with zesty Sesame-Mustard Dressing. Fold the packets and eat them like a taco—fun, flavorful finger food!

Boston lettuce leaves or leaf lettuce
1/4 cup dry white wine
1/4 teaspoon ground Szechuan peppercorns
1 (1/4-inch-thick) slice peeled fresh gingerroot, smashed
1 green onion, smashed
2 whole chicken breasts, skinned
2 teaspoons black Dry Roasted Sesame Seeds, page 24

Sesame-Mustard Dressing:
1/3 cup rice vinegar
2 teaspoons sesame seed oil
3 tablespoons sugar
2 tablespoons honey
1 teaspoon medium Japanese soy sauce
2 teaspoons Dijon-style mustard
1 teaspoon salt or to taste
Dash ground Szechuan peppercorns
3/4 cup almond or vegetable oil
1 tablespoon Dry Roasted Sesame Seeds, page 24

Eight Precious Condiments:
1 recipe Spicy Vermicelli Snack, page 69
6 green onions, smashed, shredded
1 cup fresh cilantro leaves
1/2 cup toasted pine nuts, almonds or sunflower kernels
1 medium-size red bell pepper, ends trimmed, seeded, ribs removed, cut in
**   matchstick julienne strips**
1 package radish sprouts (kaiwari daikon) or alfalfa sprouts
1 European-style cucumber, ends trimmed, cut in half lengthwise, seeded, cut in
**   matchstick julienne strips**
2 medium-size carrots, thinly sliced diagonally, cut in matchstick julienne strips

Rinse and dry lettuce; refrigerate in zip-type plastic storage bags until needed. In a medium-size round glass baking dish, combine wine, peppercorns, gingerroot and green onion. Add chicken breasts, meat-side-down. Let stand at room temperature 30 minutes. In a wok or deep pot, bring about 4 cups water to a boil. Place dish of chicken on a steamer tray. Cover tray with foil; place over boiling water. Steam chicken 20 minutes or until done. Remove tray from heat. Let chicken cool in marinade 1 hour.

Prepare Sesame-Mustard Dressing. With fingers, shred chicken into a medium-size bowl. Toss chicken with 2 to 3 tablespoons of Sesame-Mustard Dressing. Pour remaining dressing into a serving bowl. Mound chicken in middle of a serving platter. Sprinkle with black Dry Roasted Sesame Seeds. Arange Eight Precious

Condiments around chicken. Serve with lettuce. Invite guests to place a small amount of shredded chicken in center of a lettuce leaf. Top with small amounts of desired condiments. Spoon on dressing and fold lettuce leaf, enclosing ingredients inside. Eat like a taco. Makes 8 servings.

Sesame-Mustard Dressing:
In a blender or food processor fitted with the steel blade, process all ingredients except almond oil and Dry Roasted Sesame Seeds several seconds to blend. With machine running, pour almond oil slowly through feed tube, processing just until dressing is emulsified. In a medium-size bowl, combine dressing and sesame seeds. Use at once. Or cover tightly and refrigerate until needed. Makes about 1-1/3 cups.

Julienne Pear Salad with Lemon-Sesame Dressing
Korea

In the "land of the morning calm," great emphasis is placed upon the proper cutting of foods, especially vegetables. They are often cut in julienne strips which result in a confetti-like burst of color in the finished dish. This cool, yet spicy salad features the Asian apple-pear, a fabulous fruit resembling a round yellow apple with the crunchy texture of jicima and the juiciness and flavor of a ripe pear. Check local Asian markets, specialty-produce sections in supermarkets, or farmers' markets for this increasingly available fruit. If you can't find an apple-pear, substitute one or two crisp Anjou pears or jicima. (Photo on cover.)

2 to 3 carrots, thinly sliced diagonally, cut in 2-inch julienne strips
1 European-style cucumber, ends trimmed, sliced in 2-inch lengths, cut in
    julienne strips
1 large apple-pear, peeled, sliced, cut in 2-inch julienne strips
6 green onions, smashed, flattened, shredded
1/2 medium-size red bell pepper, cut in 2-inch julienne strips
1/2 medium-size green bell pepper, cut in 2-inch julienne strips
1 teaspoon Korean red pepper threads (shile kochu) or 1/2 teaspoon dried red
    pepper flakes
3 to 4 Boston lettuce leaves or red leaf lettuce leaves, shredded
1 heaping tablespoon black Dry Roasted Sesame Seeds, page 24
Additional lettuce leaves

Lemon-Sesame Dressing:
1/4 cup fresh lemon juice
1/2 teaspoon sesame seed oil
2 heaping tablespoons sugar or to taste
1/2 teaspoon salt
Freshly grated peel 1 large lemon

Place carrots, cucumber, apple-pear, green onions, bell peppers, red pepper threads, shredded lettuce and black Dry Roasted Sesame Seeds in a large bowl. Prepare Lemon-Sesame Dressing; pour over vegetable mixture. Combine well. Cover and refrigerate 1 hour. Line a serving platter with additional lettuce leaves. Toss salad in dressing again. Spoon onto serving platter. Serve at once. Makes 6 servings.

Lemon-Sesame Dressing:
In a small bowl, combine all ingredients. Blend well until sugar is dissolved. Makes 1/3 cup.

Cinnamon-Scented Roast Duck Salad in Egg-Flour Wrappers

Malaysia

Fresh-style spring rolls are a special occasion food, enjoyed in countries throughout Southeast Asia. In Malaysia, they are called "poh-pia," meaning thin skin or pancake in Chinese. The filling is sometimes wrapped with the delicate wheat-flour skins favored by the Chinese, but golden egg-flour wrappers add a distinctively Malaysian touch. For an economical and versatile substitute for duck, try roasting bone-in turkey parts such as drumsticks, hindquarters or thighs.

1 (4-1/2- to 5-lb.) duck, thawed if frozen
3 stalks fresh lemongrass or strips of peel 2 lemons
1 tablespoon vegetable oil
2 (2-inch) cinnamon sticks, broken
2 shallots, thinly sliced
1/2 teaspoon whole cloves
1/2 teaspoon five-spice powder
3 (1/4-inch-thick) slices fresh gingerroot, smashed
Salt
Black pepper
1 recipe Plum Brandy Sauce, page 136
1 recipe Orange-Flavored Bean Sauce, page 139
1 recipe Crispy Fried Onions, page 26

Garden Greenery:
Fresh leaf lettuce, torn in small pieces
1 European-style cucumber, ends trimmed, cut in half, seeded, cut in 2-inch
    julienne strips
6 green onions, smashed, shredded
1 small yellow bell pepper, ends trimmed, seeded, ribs removed, cut in 2-inch
    julienne strips
1 cup fresh cilantro leaves

Egg-Flour Wrappers:
3 large eggs
2 tablespoons vegetable oil
1 cup water
3/4 cup cornstarch
1/3 cup flour
1/4 teaspoon salt

Preheat oven to 450F (230C). Trim excess fat from duck in neck area and near tail. Place duck on a rack in a heavy roasting pan. If using lemongrass, remove tough outer stalks. Crush remaining portion of stalks; cut in 3-inch pieces. In a wok or a large skillet, heat oil over medium-high heat until hot. Add lemongrass or lemon peel, cinnamon, shallots, cloves, five-spice powder and gingerroot. Cook, stirring constantly, 1 to 2 minutes or until aromatic. Spoon mixture into cavity of duck.

To prepare **Cinnamon-Scented Roast Duck Salad in Egg-Flour Wrappers**, *spoon aromatic spices into the cavity of the duck and roast until a mouth-watering golden-brown.*

Spread a golden egg-flour wrapper with a tasty sauce and top with fresh garden greenery and succulent roast duck. Fold the golden skin to inclose the small portable salad.

With a trussing needle, carefully pierce fatty skin to let fat drain off while roasting. Sprinkle outside of duck with salt and black pepper. Roast in preheated oven on middle rack 45 to 50 minutes. Remove fat from pan juices 1 to 2 times while roasting. Prepare Garden Greenery and Egg-Flour Wrappers. Remove duck from oven and cool 10 minutes. Pour any spiced juices inside duck back into roasting pan. Stir pan juices into dipping sauces for flavor enrichment, if desired. To slice duck, cut off legs and thighs at thigh joint. Carve breast in small slices. Carve as much meat as possible from legs and thighs; pull remaining meat off with fingers.

Arrange duck on a platter. Crisp duck skin under a broiler, if desired, and add to platter. Serve duck with Garden Greenery, Egg-Flour Wrappers, Plum Brandy Sauce, Orange-Flavored Bean Sauce and Crispy Fried Onions. Invite each guest to spread a wrapper with 1 to 2 teaspoons of desired sauce. Add a small amount of greenery, duck, fried onions and additional sauce, if desired. Fold sides of wrapper over ingredients. Make 6 to 8 servings.

Garden Greenery:
Arrange all ingredients on a serving platter.

Egg-Flour Wrappers:
In a medium-size bowl, whisk eggs, oil and water. Stir in dry ingredients until smooth. Let stand 15 minutes. Heat a crepe pan over medium-low heat. If pan is not nonstick, wipe with vegetable oil. Pour 2 tablespoons of batter into pan. At same time, lift pan with opposite hand and roll around so batter will thinly coat bottom of pan. Cook 1 minute or just until bottom of wrapper is set. Edges will begin to slightly brown and lift. Adjust heat to prevent wrappers from cooking too fast or too slow, if necessary. Flip wrapper over; cook 30 seconds. Transfer to a platter to cool. Repeat with remaining batter, stacking wrappers on platter. Fold wrappers in quarters. Cover until needed. Makes 16 wrappers.

HINT
Garden Greenery can be prepared up to 1 day ahead and refrigerated in zip-type plastic bags. Egg-Flour Wrappers can be made several hours ahead and stacked between sheets of plastic wrap; keep covered at room temperature.

Shrimp & Kiwifruit in
Lemon-Kimizu Dressing

Japan

I have substituted the tang of fresh lemon juice for the usual rice vinegar used in this delicate cooked-egg dressing. In the word "kimizu," "kimi" refers to the egg yolk, and "zu," the vinegar. This type of salad falls into the category of "Aemono," meaning the composed salad is gently blanketed with a delicate, slightly thickened dressing. Fresh crab heralds the beginning of winter in Japan. It's a perfect partner for the immensely popular kiwifruit. I treasure memories of shopping at Japanese street markets and bringing home one or two large bagfuls of inexpensive, plump kiwifruits each trip. We peeled and ate them, western-style, as casually as if we were eating apples. (Photo on cover.)

**1 Japanese cucumber or 1/2 European-style cucumber, ends trimmed, cut in half
    lengthwise, seeded, cut crosswise in paper-thin slices**
2 teaspoons salt
6 shiso leaves
3 chilled kiwifruits, peeled, sliced
**1/2 pound medium-size shrimp, cooked, peeled, deveined, lump crabmeat or
    poached bay scallops**
Fresh enokitake (snow puff) mushrooms

Lemon-Kimizu Dressing:
1 large egg yolk
1/4 cup plus 2 tablespoons sugar
1/2 teaspoon salt
1 tablespoon cornstarch
3 tablespoons fresh lemon juice
3 tablespoons water
1/4 teaspoon sesame seed oil
1 to 2 teaspoons hot water, if needed

Prepare Lemon-Kimizu Dressing. In a small bowl, cover cucumber with a small amount of cold water. Add salt. Soak 20 minutes or until cucumber slices soften. Drain well, pressing out all moisture. Arrange shiso leaves on a serving platter or on individual serving plates. Place a mound of cucumber on each shiso leaf. Arrange kiwifruit slices and shrimp on shiso leaves. Top each with 1 generous tablespoon of Lemon-Kimizu Dressing. Garnish with enokitake mushrooms. Serve at once. Makes 6 servings.

Lemon-Kimizu Dressing:
In a small bowl, beat egg yolk with a small whisk or fork. In a small saucepan, combine sugar, salt, cornstarch, lemon juice and 3 tablespoons water. Cook, stirring constantly, over medium heat until thickened. Stir in sesame seed oil. Whisk hot dressing into beaten egg yolk gradually until sauce is thickened. If dressing is too thick, add enough hot water to thin dressing to desired consistency. Serve at room temperature. Makes about 1/2 cup.

FINGER FOODS & SNACKS

The Asian people are avid snackers. They do enjoy a structured system of eating two to three basic meals daily, but are given to supplementing them with numerous little dishes eaten at intervals during the span of a day. Snacking is a social and cultural phenomenon in Asia. Few cultures devote as much leisure time to food. The Asian people are extremely sociable and feel that food is meant to be shared and not eaten alone. Snacks are instinctively served to satisfy hunger, but more importantly they are associated with times of fellow communion—when greeting friends, conducting business or celebrating a social occasion. And of course, tea drinking requires the presence of snacks.

In Asia, snack foods are often eaten outside the home. In Malaysia, Indonesia and Singapore, businessmen gather in coffee shops to drink coffee or tea and enjoy eating snacks. All through Asia, one can purchase delicious, hearty snacks from street vendors or at street stalls.

An entire category of hearty snack foods can be found in the famous teahouses of Southern China. One goes to a teahouse in the morning to take "yum cha," which translated means to "drink tea." The delightful teahouse foods are called "dim sum." Translated, that means "dot on the heart," or perhaps a more poetic connotation would be "small pleasures of the heart." You can find appropriate snacks for a Chinese tea lunch in this chapter as well as in many of the other chapters throughout the book. Long ago, Cantonese chefs devised an entire group of foods which are now teahouse classics. The old favorites will always be around, but today's chefs are creating new teahouse offerings. In the spirit of teahouse foods, you can delight your family and friends with cross-cultural "small pleasures of the heart" such as the Malaysian Spicy Pork with Bamboo Shoots in Pastry Baskets, pages 84-85. These are often served in Malaysia during afternoon tea.

Japan's snack contribution to the world is "sushi," (lightly sweetened, vinegared rice). Glazed Walnut Sushi Roll, pages 76-77, can be served as a snack or as a light and satisfying lunch.

Sweets in Asia are usually served as between-meal snacks with hot tea, never as the final course of a meal. Many pastries in the Sweet Temptations chapter could be served this way.

Hearty Asian snacks are so versatile they can be served as part of a multicourse meal or appetizers for oriental or western meals. Most of them can be made ahead of time and refrigerated or frozen.

Crispy Fried Tofu Nuggets
with Condiments

Korea

Tofu is a food whose time has come. Health conscious consumers know that tofu is high in protein, vitamins and calcium. Throughout the Orient, people have known the value of this ancient health food for centuries. In Korea, tofu is fried, added to soups and combined with meats and vegetables. Potato starch makes the coating extra crispy. The insides remain creamy and smooth.

1 chilled European-style cucumber, peeled

Tofu Nuggets:
1 (16- to 20-oz.) package firm Chinese-style tofu
3 cups peanut or vegetable oil for deep-frying
1/2 cup potato starch or cornstarch, more if needed

Condiments:
1 recipe Spicy Soy Sauce Dip, page 140
1 heaping tablespoon Dry Roasted Sesame Seeds, page 24
4 green onions, smashed, flattened, slivered
1 tablespoon grated fresh gingerroot
2 tablespoons grated Japanese white radish (daikon)

Cut cucumber in half lengthwise. With a spoon, remove seeds. Cut halves crosswise in 1/2-inch-thick slices. Spread cucumber slices over a serving platter. Refrigerate until needed. Prepare Tofu Nuggets and Condiments. Place Tofu Nuggets on top of cucumbers. Serve at once with Condiments. Invite guests to season individual bowls of Spicy Soy Sauce Dip with Condiments. Spoon dip over Tofu Nuggets and cucumbers. Makes 4 to 5 servings.

Tofu Nuggets:
Cut tofu horizontally in 1-inch-thick slices. Lay slices between double layers of kitchen towels or several layers of paper towels. Place 1 pound of weight on top 5 minutes to press out excess liquid and firm tofu.

In a wok or shallow heavy saucepan, heat oil to 360F (180C) or until a 1-inch cube of bread turns golden-brown in 60 seconds. Cut tofu in 1-inch cubes; coat with potato starch. Fry tofu in several batches until golden-brown and crispy. Drain on a wire rack. To insure crispness, tofu can be fried again. Heat oil to 375F (190C). Fry tofu in 2 batches, about 45 seconds per batch. Drain well.

Condiments:
Serve Spicy Soy Sauce Dip in individual serving bowls. Serve remaining condiments separately in small dishes.

HINT
The first frying can be done 1 to 2 hours ahead. Do not refrigerate. Fry second time just before serving.

Spicy Vermicelli Snack

Southeast Asian

These ultra-thin crispy noodles are made from shredded, deep-fried egg roll wrappers. They can be seasoned with your favorite spicy-hot seasoning mixtures or with other toppings such as grated Parmesan cheese, barbecue spice or garlic salt. Use them as a crunchy topping for salads or soups or just grab a handful for a delicious snack.

1 pound thin spring roll wrappers or thin won ton wrappers
6 cups peanut or vegetable oil for deep-frying
Seven-spice powder (shichimi togarashi) or seasoning salt mixed with red pepper
   (cayenne) to taste

Divide spring roll wrappers in 3 to 4 stacks. With a large sharp knife, cut each stack of wrappers in 1/8-inch-thick strips. Toss in a loose pile. In a wok or heavy saucepan, heat oil to 360F (180C) or until a 1-inch cube of bread turns golden-brown in 60 seconds. Fry shredded vermicelli in 3 to 4 batches until golden-brown and crisp. Drain on paper towels. Immediately sprinkle with seven-spice powder. Cool and serve at once. Or store in an airtight container up to 2 weeks. Makes topping for 8 to 10 salad servings or 4 snack servings.

Some recipes in this cookbook call for lemongrass, green onions, sliced gingerroot or unpeeled garlic cloves to be smashed before using. To smash the vegetable, lay it on a cutting board. With the broad side of a cleaver or a chef's knife, hit the vegetable with a forceful whack. The fibers of the flattened vegetable will be broken and the juice released to provide more flavor. The garlic skins will loosen and can be removed, eliminating tedious peeling. Use the vegetable as is or mince according to recipe directions. Smashing the vegetable will make mincing easier.

Chinese Firecrackers　　　　　　　*China*

In China, the beginning of the New Year celebration is heralded by the explosion of as many as 100,000 burning firecrackers! In old China, it was believed that the loud explosion made by the firecrackers would scare away evil spirits. Start your own Chinese New Year celebration with a bang and serve these edible firecrackers made with tissue-thin pastry, deliciously stuffed with a spicy-hot filling of pork and shrimp. The filling can be made one to two days ahead. Shaped firecrackers can be wrapped tightly and refrigerated several hours before baking. Serve the firecrackers with Chinese mustard and Apricot Sauce, Curried Lamb Crescents with Pine Nuts & Apricot Sauce, page 44, or Garlic & Vinegar Dipping Sauce, page 140. (Photo on cover.)

2 medium-size dried shiitake mushrooms
2 tablespoons soy sauce
1 tablespoon ground fresh chili paste (sambal oelek) or chili paste with garlic
2 to 3 teaspoons cornstarch
1/2 pound lean ground pork or veal or skinned boned ground chicken breast
　(about 1 tightly packed cup)
2 tablespoons dry white wine
1/2 pound raw shrimp, peeled, deveined, finely chopped
3/4 cup vegetable oil or as needed
2 garlic cloves, finely minced
1 teaspoon finely minced fresh gingerroot
3 green onions, finely minced
3 cups finely shredded cabbage
1 small carrot, shredded
10 sheets filo dough
1 tablespoon sesame seed oil or as needed

In a small bowl, cover mushrooms with warm water. Soak 30 minutes. Squeeze mushrooms dry. Reserve 2 tablespoons of soaking liquid. Cut off and discard tough stems; mince mushrooms finely. In a small bowl, combine reserved soaking liquid, 1 tablespoon of soy sauce, chili paste and 1 teaspoon of cornstarch. In another small bowl, combine remaining soy sauce and cornstarch, ground meat and 1 tablespoon of wine. Let stand 10 minutes.

In another small bowl, combine shrimp and remaining wine. Heat a wok or large skillet over high heat until hot. Add 2 tablespoons of oil. When oil is hot, add garlic and gingerroot; stir-fry 5 seconds. Add ground meat mixture; stir-fry 1 minute or until meat is no longer pink. Add shrimp and wine; stir-fry 30 seconds or until shrimp is pink. Remove mixture to a platter. Wipe excess moisture from wok with paper towels. Reheat wok; add 2 tablespoons of oil. Add minced mushrooms, green onions, cabbage and carrot; stir-fry about 2 minutes or until crisp-tender. Return meat-shrimp mixture to wok; reduce heat. Push filling mixture aside. Restir soy sauce mixture; pour into wok. Cook until juices are thickened; stir into filling. Cool filling.

Preheat oven to 375F (190C). Place 1 filo sheet on a flat surface. Cover remaining sheets to prevent drying. In a small bowl, combine remaining 1/2 cup vegetable oil with sesame seed oil; prepare more as needed. Brush top side of filo sheet with oil mixture. Place another filo sheet on top of oiled sheet. Brush with oil. Cut sheets in 4 equal pieces. Place 2 tablespoons of filling near front edge of 1 piece of filo; shape in a 3-inch log. With pinking shears, trim sides of filo near ends of log-shaped filling. Beginning at side nearest filling, roll filo in a cylinder, enclosing filling. Firmly press filo near ends of filling to form firecracker ends.

Place crumpled pieces of foil inside trimmed ends to hold open so shapes can set during baking. Brush firecrackers lightly with oil mixture. Place on a baking sheet; cover lightly to prevent drying. Repeat with remaining ingredients. Bake in preheated oven 18 to 20 minutes or until pastry is crisp and golden-brown. Cover ends with foil if they brown too quickly. Makes 18 to 20 firecrackers.

*To prepare **Chinese Firecrackers**, spoon a spicy-hot filling of pork, shrimp and vegetables on a piece of filo dough brushed with oil. Roll the filo dough in a cylinder and crimp the ends to form a "firecracker."*

Deep-Fried Shrimp Chips

These brightly colored, translucent dried wafers are made of a pureed seafood and starch mixure. When deep-fried, they puff up in large pastel-colored crisp chips. Be sure and store uncooked shrimp chips in a dry place or they may not puff properly when deep-fried. They are quite tasty and will add a flowerlike rainbow-colored garnishment to your table. They are a great accompaniment to salads or can be used as dippers in place of potato chips. (Photo on page 79.)

> **Peanut or vegetable oil for deep-frying**
> **1 box shrimp chips**

In a wok or shallow heavy saucepan, heat oil to 400F (205C) or until a 1-inch cube of bread turns golden-brown in 20 seconds. Fry several shrimp chips at a time. They will sink into oil, bob back to top, then puff up in large opaque pastel-colored shapes. Drain on paper towels. Serve at once. Or store in an airtight container up to 2 days. Makes 1 box shrimp chips.

> *HINT*
> *Chips can be refreshed in a preheated 350F (175C) oven.*

Crunchy Potato & Peanut Snack   *India/Pakistan*

Indian markets are filled with an endless variety of savory, crunchy fried potato, lentil and noodle snacks. This spicy, crisp golden potato snack can be quickly made in about five minutes, and will usually last about the same length of time! A great snack for parties, camping trips or while traveling.

2 tablespoons vegetable oil
1 teaspoon ground cumin
1 teaspoon ground tumeric
1 (7-oz.) can shoestring potato sticks
1 (8-oz.) jar dry roasted peanuts
1/4 teaspon red pepper (cayenne)

In a large pan, heat oil over medium heat until hot. Stir cumin and tumeric quickly into oil. Mix in potato sticks until golden and aromatic. Stir in peanuts and sprinkle with red pepper. Cool mixture. Store in an airtight container. Makes about 4-1/2 cups.

VARIATION

To prepare *Indonesian-Style Crunchy Potato & Peanut Snack*, add 1/2 teaspoon ground allspice to hot oil with cumin and tumeric. Substitute 1 recipe Crispy Fried Onions with Coconut & Peanuts, page 126, for peanuts.

To prepare *Chinese-Style Crunchy Potato & Peanut Snack*, omit cumin. Substitute 1 recipe Five-Spice Nuts, page 129, for peanuts.

Pressed Rice Cakes

Malaysia

Pressed cooked rice is a favorite food throughout Southeast Asia. In Malaysia rice is cooked in hollow bamboo poles or in small packets intricately woven from young bamboo leaves. A simpler Malaysian method for making pressed rice is "nasi himpit"—cooked rice is pressed into a pan, then cut in cubes. It is traditionally served with satay (skewered grilled meats and seafood). The rice cakes provide a soothing taste contrast when accompanied by Satay Peanut Sauce, page 138. Rice cakes are also served with curried meat dishes and with soups. Cold rice cakes are delicious dipped into beaten egg white, coated with "panko" (Japanese-style bread crumbs) and deep fried. To serve, line a flat basket or tray with ti or banana leaves. Place rice cubes on the leaves. (Photo on page 115.)

> 2 cups long-grain jasmine rice or other long-grain rice
> 3 cups water
> 1 teaspoon salt

Rinse rice in a large bowl of cool water, removing any foreign material. Pour off milky water. Continue rising until water runs clear. Drain in a fine strainer. In a medium-size bowl, cover rice with water; soak overnight. Drain rice.

In a medium-size saucepan, bring rice, 3 cups water and salt to a boil over high heat. Reduce heat to low, cover and simmer 20 minutes. Remove from heat. Let stand, covered and undisturbed, 10 minutes. Firmly press rice in an even layer in a 13'' x 9'' dish. Cover surface with plastic wrap. Set a smaller rectangular pan on top, then place 1 pound of weight inside smaller pan. Refrigerate at least 6 hours or overnight. Remove from refrigerator 1 hour before serving. Cut in 1-1/2-inch cubes. Makes about 12 servings

VARIATIONS

To prepare *Pressed Coconut Rice Cakes*, substitute 2 cups Light Coconut Milk, page 21, for 2 cups of water.

Substitute short-grain rice for long-grain rice. Reduce liquid to 2-1/2 cups.

In China, India, Thailand, Viet Nam, the Philippines and the East Indies, indica or firm long-grain rice is preferred because it cooks up in separate fluffy grains. California grown long-grain rice has a more tender grain, closer in composition to long-grain rice grown in Asia. In Japan, Korea and occasionally the Philippines, Japonica rice, which has a softer, more cohesive medium-grain to short-grain, is preferred.

Perfumed jasmine rice from Thailand and aged scented basmati rice from Northern India are excellent types of aromatic long-grain rice. White or brown texmati rice from Texas is a new strain combining the characteristics of long-grain rice and basmati. Calmati is a nutritious new brown basmati from California.

Store rice in an airtight container in a cool, dry place. Aromatic rice will not keep as long as regular long-grain rice. Refrigerate for longer storage, up to 10 months.

Picnic Box Stuffed Chicken Rolls

Japan

One of the handicrafts I admire most in Japan is the exquisite art of food packaging. From the simple, natural packaging of a single perfect leaf wrapped around a rice cake to intricate folded paper boxes tied with silken cords, the Japanese present us with evidence of their philosophy that all things small or large are indeed significant and beautiful. Portable box meals have a long treasured history in Japan. Called "bento," they began as simple packets of cooked rice and pickles carried to the fields by farmers and by soldiers on long campaigns. Today they are carried by businessmen, school children, travelers and picnickers. They are packaged in containers ranging from simple wood or paper to handcrafted baskets to lacquer, pottery or paper boxes. "Bento" foods are prepared in advance and eaten at room temperature. They are composed of the freshest seasonal foods with a seasonal motif. Present your favorite "bento" foods in regional American baskets, pottery or gaily decorated boxes or tins. An authority on entertaining "bento-style," Japanese embassy wife Mrs. Masako Wakabayashi shared this easy do-ahead recipe for baked chicken rolls. When sliced, the centers reveal colorful vegetables. Masako often includes sliced chicken rolls in special "bentos" prepared at her home in Washington, D.C. for western guests and visiting dignitaries from Japan.

4 chicken breast halves, skinned, boned, slightly flattened
2 tablespoons sake
2 tablespoons light or medium Japanese soy sauce
1 tablespoon fresh ginger juice
4 small green onions
1 large carrot, cut in 4 strips, blanched 1 minute
1/2 small red bell pepper, ends trimmed, seeded, ribs removed, cut in
   1/2-inch-wide strips
1 stalk celery, cut in 4 strips
Salt to taste
Seven-spice powder (shichimi togarashi), sansho pepper or black pepper to taste

Score chicken breasts lightly on both sides; place in a large baking dish. Sprinkle with sake, soy sauce and ginger juice. Cover tightly. Let stand at least 2 hours or overnight. Preheat oven to 350F (175C). Drain chicken. Trim vegetables to width of chicken breasts. Place 1 green onion and 1 strip each of carrot, bell pepper and celery in middle of each chicken breast. Sprinkle with salt and seven-spice powder. Roll up chicken enclosing vegetables. Secure openings with short bamboo skewers. Bake in preheated oven 22 to 25 minutes. Cool and slice in 1/2-inch-thick slices. Or cover uncut rolls and refrigerate up to 8 hours. Makes 10 to 12 servings.

Clockwise from top left on plate; Miniature tomatoes and carrots; Szechuan Marinated Vegetables, page 132; Picnic Box Stuffed Chicken Rolls; Glazed Walnut Sushi Roll, pages 76-77

Glazed Walnut Sushi Roll

Japan

A "futomaki" (thick sushi roll) is a smorgasbord of ingredients wrapped in seasoned rice and crisp laver, nutritious black sheets of a sea vegetable the Japanese call "nori." Usually filled with six to eight ingredients, a "futomaki" lends itself to improvisation. Experiment with a variety of seafood, meats, vegetables and pickles. The sweet-savory glazed walnuts give this vegetarian sushi roll a rich, almost meaty taste, and add appealing crunch to every bite. Not overly sweet, the candy-like nuts make a chewy, delicious snack. (Photo on page 75.)

1 (3/4- to 1-oz.) package dried gourd strip (kampyo)
2 teaspoons salt
1 recipe Glazing Sauce, Sake-Glazed Mushrooms, page 46
1/2 cup water
2 tablespoons rice vinegar
5 (8- x 7-1/2-inch) sheets nori, toasted
1 recipe Sushi Rice, page 23
1 tablespoon plus 2 teaspoons prepared Japanese horseradish (wasabi)
1 recipe Steamed Egg Cake with Green Onion, page 81, cut in
   1/2-inch-wide strips
1 recipe Sake-Glazed Mushrooms, page 46, sliced
1 recipe Lemon-Cucumber Sunomono, page 131, or sliced Japanese pickle
10 asparagus stalks, if desired, peeled, ends trimmed, steamed until tender
1 tablespoon plus 2 teaspoons Dry Roasted Sesame Seeds, page 24
Pink pickled ginger slices (amazu shoga)

Teriyaki Glazed Walnuts:
1-1/2 cups walnut halves
1/4 cup light corn syrup
2 tablespoons medium Japanese soy sauce
2 tablespoons light-brown sugar

Prepare Teriyaki Glazed Walnuts. In a small bowl, cover gourd strip with water; add salt. Soak 20 minutes to soften fibers. Drain and rinse well. Cut in 8-inch strips. In a small saucepan, simmer gourd strips in Glazing Sauce until sauce is completely reduced. Cool gourd strips. In a small bowl, combine water and rice vinegar for moistening hands. Place 1 sheet of nori, shiny side face down and long side running horizontally, on edge of a bamboo sushi mat.

With a damp measuring cup, measure 1 cup Sushi Rice; unmold in middle of nori sheet. With damp hands, press rice over nori, leaving 1-3/4 inches uncovered at top. Make a slight horizontal indentation along center of rice from end to end. Spread indentation with 1 teaspoon of horseradish. Place 1/5 of Teriyaki Glazed Walnuts, gourd strips, Steamed Egg Cake with Green Onion, Sake-Glazed Mushrooms, Lemon-Cucumber Sunomono and 2 asparagus stalks, if desired, along length of horseradish. Sprinkle with 1 teaspoon of Dry Roasted Sesame Seeds.

To form roll, lift edge of mat with thumbs. Hold ingredients in place with fingers and roll mat and nori to enclose filling. Roll to far edge of rice, leaving uncovered portion of nori extended. Tuck in escaping grains. Press mat firmly to set shape. Moisten extending edge of nori with water; complete roll. Wrap mat completely around rice roll; press gently a few seconds. Unroll, tap ends on counter to even. Repeat with remaining ingredients.

*To prepare **Glazed Walnut Sushi Roll**, place a sheet of nori on a bamboo sushi mat. Press the prepared rice over the nori and add the vegetarian filling. Holding the filling ingredients in place, roll the mat and nori away from you to enclose the filling.*

Place rolls on a cutting surface, seam-side down. Wet a large sharp knife with water-vinegar mixture. Slice rolls in half; wipe and dampen knife between cuts. Slice each half in 3 (1-1/4-inch) pieces. Place on a serving tray with small piles of pickled ginger slices. Or store uncut in a loosely covered rectangular pan several hours at room temperature. Do not refrigerate. Makes 30 pieces.

Teriyaki Glazed Walnuts:
Bring a small pot filled with water to a boil. Add nuts; remove pan from heat. Let stand 30 minutes. Preheat oven to 250F (120 C). Drain nuts. Pat dry on paper towels. Spread nuts on a baking sheet. Bake in preheated oven 20 minutes or until completely dry and toasted. Oil a baking sheet or large pan. In a small saucepan, combine corn syrup, soy sauce and brown sugar. Simmer over medium-low heat 1 minute. Stir in walnuts until well coated. Cook, stirring constantly, 1 to 2 minutes or until walnuts completely absorb syrup and start becoming slightly tacky. Scrape nuts onto oiled baking sheet; spread in a flat layer. When cool, break apart. Makes 1-1/2 cups.

Crispy Potato Julienne with
Red Pepper & Green Onion Sauce

Korea

In Korea, street vendors stroll through city streets pushing large carts of golden fried potato-strips. At first, this recipe may remind you of eating french fries with ketchup, but with your first taste, you will realize the flavorful difference. Crispy-fried julienne-cut potatoes are served with a flavorful, tart sauce based on spicy "kochu jang" (Korean red bean paste). Serve the sauce for dipping or mix the sauce with the potatoes. This can be served as a side dish or savor the flavors and serve small portions as an appetizer course.

**5 medium-size potatoes, peeled, cut in 1/4-inch-thick slices, slices cut in
  1/4-inch-wide strips
1-1/2 cups peanut or vegetable oil
3 tablespoons sesame seed oil
1/2 teaspoon salt or to taste
1/4 teaspoon red pepper (cayenne)
1/4 teaspoon black pepper
1 strip red bell pepper, diced
1 green onion stem, chopped
1 teaspoon black Dry Roasted Sesame Seeds, page 24
3 green onion stems, if desired, shredded**

**Red-Pepper & Green Onion Sauce:
1/4 cup Korean red-pepper paste (kochu jang)
2 tablespoons rice vinegar
1/2 teaspoon sesame seed oil
2 teaspoons Dry Roasted Sesame Seeds, page 24
1 teaspoon sugar
1 large green onion, finely minced**

In a large bowl of water, soak cut potatoes 15 minutes. Prepare Red-Pepper & Green Onion Sauce. Drain potatoes well. Pat dry on paper towels. In a large heavy skillet or an electric skillet, heat peanut oil and sesame seed oil over high heat to 375F (190C) or until a 1-inch cube of bread turns golden-brown in 50 seconds. Fry potatoes, turning often, 8 to 10 minutes or until crispy and golden-brown. Sprinkle potatoes with salt and peppers. Remove from hot oil. Drain on paper towels. Sprinkle with bell pepper, chopped green onion stem and black Dry Roasted Sesame Seeds. Garnish with shredded green onion stems, if desired. Serve with Red-Pepper & Green Onion Sauce for dipping. Makes 4 servings.

Red-Pepper Sauce & Green Onion Sauce:
In a small bowl, combine all ingredients. Makes about 1/2 cup.

Clockwise from upper right: Crispy Potato Julienne with Red Pepper & Green Onion Sauce; Deep-Fried Shrimp Chips, page 71; Spicy Pork with Bamboo Shoots in Pastry Baskets, pages 84-85

Shrimp & Onion Fritters

Japan

Japanese Navy wife Kyoko Shiga taught me how to make her special shrimp fritters. The shrimp and vegetables are cut up and mixed into the batter. The fritters are crispy and at their best eaten shortly after being fried. But unlike tempura, they can wait one to two hours before being served. The delicious fried crispy bits of leftover batter are called "age-dama." Save them and sprinkle on soups, noodle dishes or add to the Japanese-Style Pizza batter, pages 104-105.

20 raw large shrimp (about 1 lb.), peeled, deveined, each cut in 4 pieces
1 medium-size onion, cut in quarters, thinly sliced
1/2 medium-size carrot, thinly sliced diagonally, cut in 1-inch julienne strips
1 small green bell pepper, ends trimmed, seeded, ribs removed, cut in
   1/2-inch-square pieces
1 large egg
1 cup sparkling water or tap water
1 cup cake flour
1/2 teaspoon baking powder
1/2 teaspoon salt
6 cups peanut or vegetable oil for deep-frying

In a medium-size bowl, combine shrimp, onion, carrot and bell pepper. In another medium-size bowl, slightly beat egg; stir in water, flour, baking powder and salt just until blended, then stir in shrimp mixture. In a wok or shallow heavy saucepan, heat oil to 360F (180C) or until a 1-inch cube of bread turns golden-brown in 60 seconds. Fry tablespoonfuls of batter, turning occasionally, 3 to 4 minutes or until crispy and golden-brown. Drain on paper towels. Makes 6 servings.

HINT
Skim oil several times. Reserve crispy bits of fried batter. Drizzle any remaining batter into hot oil. Serve crispy bits with fritters or reserve for another use.

Steamed Egg Cake with Green Onion   *Japan*

Steamed Egg Cake with Green Onion is a delicious addition to Glazed Walnut Sushi Roll, pages 76-77, or can be eaten as a nutritious snack. Vary the flavor by adding two tablespoons spinach or watercress puree or try substituting "nira" (Japanese chives) or regular chives for the green onion. The egg cake is especially tasty when quickly sautéed lightly on both sides in hot vegetable oil.

> **3 extra-large eggs**
> **1 tablespoon Japanese sweet rice wine (mirin)**
> **1 teaspoon sugar**
> **Scant 1/8 teaspoon salt**
> **1 small green onion, finely minced**

Oil an 8 '' x 4 '' glass loaf pan. In a medium-size bowl, whisk all ingredients. Pour into oiled pan. In a wok or deep pot, bring 4 cups water to a boil. Place pan on a steamer tray and cover. Place tray over boiling water. Reduce heat to medium-high. Steam 5 to 6 minutes or until egg cake is set. Cool 5 minutes. Remove from pan. Cut in 16 (2- x 1-inch) strips. Makes 16 pieces.

In Japan rice was once considered the standard of wealth. The Japanese prefer to eat tender, cohesive short-grain rice and use it for making "sushi" (sweet-vinegared rice). Store raw rice in an airtight container in a cool, dry place. Rice is best eaten within six months, but will keep up to one year. Rice will require addition of more water as it ages. Starchy glutinous rice should be purchased in small amounts and kept refrigerated since it becomes stale much more quickly. Raw rice should be cooked as needed.

Spanish-Style Chicken Pies with Laurel Leaf Pastry

Philippines

"Pastel," a savory deep-dish pie, is a delicious example of the culinary legacy Spain endowed upon the Philippines after centuries of colonial rule. "Pastilitos" are individual-size pies. These are filled with chicken, Spanish sausage, vegetables, raisins and chopped sweet pickles bound in a rich brown sauce. Vinegar-based pickle juice helps tenderize the pastry and aids in browning. Decorative garlands of pastry laurel leaves decorate the tops. "Pastilitos" might be served during "merienda sienna," the Filipino late afternoon high-tea. Serve these pies as a main course topped with a rich brown sauce or eat them out-of-hand as a hearty snack. (Photo on page 61.)

1 recipe Basic Tender Butter Pastry, page 27
2 tablespoons sweet gerkin pickle juice or 1 teaspoon rice vinegar
1 teaspoon ground oregano, if desired
3 tablespoons olive oil
1 (2-1/2- to 3-lb.) broiler-fryer, cut up
1 medium-size red Bermuda onion, chopped
2 large garlic cloves, finely minced
1-1/2 teaspoons all-purpose flour
1-3/4 cups chicken stock
1 medium-size potato, peeled, cut in 3/4-inch cubes
1 medium-size carrot, cut in 1/2-inch-thick slices, slices cut in quarters
1 bay leaf
1 teaspoon salt
1/2 teaspoon black pepper
1/4 pound chorizo de bilbao or linguica, casing removed, chopped, sautéed, or
   kielbasa sausage, casing removed, cut in 1/2-inch cubes
1/4 cup chopped olives
1/4 cup finely chopped sweet gerkin pickles
1/4 cup raisins
1 (2-oz.) jar chopped pimentos, drained
2 hard-cooked eggs, diced
1/4 cup frozen green peas, thawed
1 teaspoon medium Japanese soy sauce
1 teaspoon red wine vinegar
1 large egg, slightly beaten

Prepare Basic Tender Butter Pastry substituting sweet pickle juice for 2 tablespoons iced water. Add oregano to liquid, if desired. Chill pastry until needed.

In a large skillet, heat olive oil over medium-high heat. Sauté chicken until well-browned. Remove chicken. Fry onion and garlic 10 minutes or until golden-brown. Reduce heat, if necessary, to prevent burning. Add flour. Cook, stirring constantly, 1 minute. Stir in chicken stock. Add potato, carrot, bay leaf, salt and black pepper. Return chicken to skillet. Partially cover and simmer 20 minutes or until chicken is tender. Remove from heat. Remove chicken and bay leaf from sauce; cool chicken. Add chorizo de bilbao to warm sauce. Stir in olives, pickles, raisins, pimentos, eggs, green peas, soy sauce and vinegar. Bone cooled chicken and cut in small cubes. Measure 2 cups chicken; reserve remainder for another use. Stir chicken cubes into skillet ingredients. Cool completely.

To prepare **Spanish-Style Chicken Pies with Laurel Leaf Pastry**, *spoon filling on a pastry circle. Fold in half and press the edges firmly together around the edge of the pie. Drape a long thin rope of pastry around the edge of the half-moon shape. Press the pastry leaves around the edge of the pie along the stem.*

In a small bowl, beat egg with a fork. Divide Basic Tender Butter Pastry in half. Chill 1 pastry half. On a lightly floured surface, roll pastry 1/8-inch thick. Do not stretch pastry; it could shrink during baking. Using a 6-inch round saucer, cut out 4 to 5 circles. Spoon 1/3 cup of filling on lower middle section of each circle. Fold pastry to form half-moon shapes, using beaten egg as a sealant, if necessary. Press edges firmly forming a 1/2-inch rim around cut edge of each pie. Repeat with remaining pastry half and filling. Layer pastry scraps; chill 15 minutes.

Preheat oven to 400F (205C). Reroll chilled pastry scraps. Using a bay leaf as a tracing pattern, cut 32 to 40 small leaves from pastry scraps with a small knife or leaf-shaped cutter. Roll 8 to 10 long thin ropes of pastry for stems. Drape a stem around flat cut edge of each pie. Press 4 leaves around edge of each pie along stem. Brush pies with beaten egg and chill. Place on a baking sheet. Bake in preheated oven 20 to 25 minutes or until golden-brown. Serve warm or at room temperature. Makes 8 to 10 pies.

HINT
Unbaked pies can be wrapped and refrigerated 3 to 4 hours before baking. For longer storage, wrap properly and freeze. Bake frozen pies in a preheated oven 400F (205C) about 30 to 35 minutes or until golden-brown.

Spicy Pork with Bamboo Shoots in Pastry Baskets

Malaysia

"Kueh Pie Tee," a savory-filled miniature pastry, is a popular Malaysian snack, perfect for parties or Asian-style afternoon tea. The versatile, crispy miniature pastry shells are fun and couldn't be easier to make. Serve them with an endless variety of savory or sweet fillings. Use the variation of larger Fried Pastry Baskets as edible containers for many of the salad recipes in the Starters chapter. This delicious filling is seasoned with a medley of spices. Bamboo shoots are highly prized as a textural food, adding crunch and flavor. Select bamboo shoots from tubs of water in Asian markets for the best flavor. If you purchase canned shoots, buy whole ones packed in water rather than those cut in small strips and pieces. For fun, try serving the filling in crisp paper-thin Swedish timbale shells made by dipping a timbale iron into a thin egg batter, then frying the batter-coated iron in hot oil to form the shell. (Photo on page 79.)

Miniature Fried Pastry Baskets:
6 cups peanut or vegetable oil for deep-frying
1/2 (10-oz.) package round Japanese gyoza skins (about 25 skins)

Toppings:
1 recipe Crispy Fried Shallots, Crispy Fried Onions or Crispy Fried Garlic,
    page 26
1 recipe Egg Crepe, page 24, cut in 2-inch fine shreds
1/4 pound shredded crabmeat
1/4 cup chopped macadamia nuts, Five-Spice Nuts, page 129, or peanuts
Fresh cilantro leaves, watercress or minced chives

Spicy Pork with Bamboo Shoots:
2 tablespoons vegetable oil
2 large garlic cloves, finely minced
1-1/2 teaspoons finely minced fresh gingerroot
2 shallots, finely minced
1/4 cup finely minced bamboo shoots
1/2 pound ground pork or beef
1/2 teaspoon ground cumin
1/4 teaspoon ground cinnamon
1/4 teaspoon red pepper (cayenne)
1/8 teaspoon allspice
1/8 teaspoon five-spice powder
1/8 teaspoon black pepper
1/2 teaspoon salt
1 tablespoon chicken stock or water
1 tablespoon soy sauce
1/2 teaspoon cornstarch

Prepare Miniature Fried Pastry Baskets, Toppings and Spicy Pork with Bamboo Shoots. To serve, fill each pastry basket 3/4 full with warm meat filling. Add a small amount of each topping in order listed. Serve at once. Makes about 25 filled pastry baskets.

Miniature Fried Pastry Baskets:
In a wok or deep pot, heat oil to 375F (190C) or until a 1-inch cube of bread turns golden-brown in 50 seconds. Place 1 skin in a small ladle about 3-inches in diameter. Fit a smaller ladle inside larger ladle, holding skin securely in place. Lower ladles into hot oil. Hold 15 seconds or until skin is set. Remove top ladle; cook 15 to 20 seconds more. Slip basket into oil a few seconds or until crispy and golden-brown. Drain upside down on paper towels. Repeat with remaining skins. Store in an airtight container up to several days. Makes about 25 baskets.

Toppings:
Arrange on a platter for filling pastry baskets.

Spicy Pork with Bamboo Shoots:
In a wok or medium-size skillet, heat oil over medium heat. Add garlic, gingerroot and shallots. Stir-fry 1 to 2 minutes or until soft. Add bamboo shoots; stir-fry 1 minute. Add meat; stir-fry until no longer pink. Break up large pieces of pork. Stir in cumin, cinnamon, red pepper, allspice, five-spice powder, black pepper and salt. In a small bowl, combine chicken stock, soy sauce and cornstarch. Stir into meat mixture; cook until glazed. Remove from heat. Makes about 2 cups.

VARIATION
To prepare *Fried Pastry Baskets*, lay 1 lumpia or egg roll wrapper on top of hot oil; push down into oil with back of a Chinese skimmer or large ladle. Hold wrapper in place; fry 1 minute or until set. Remove skimmer or ladle; fry a few seconds more until basket is crisp and golden-brown. Drain upside-down on paper towels. Store in an airtight container. Refresh pastry baskets in a preheated oven 350F (175C) 5 minutes.

HINT
Spicy Pork with Bamboo Shoots can be prepared ahead and refrigerated. Reheat in a wok over low heat.

When your bright and shiny wok begins to lose luster and turn black, be glad because this means your wok is on the way to becoming well-seasoned. In Asia, a sooty, blackened wok is greatly respected and holds a place of honor in the Asian kitchen. With a minimum of care, your wok will age gracefully and develop its own special character.

Yam & Peanut Cracker-Bread

This delicious, spice-scented cracker-bread is made with fresh yam and a compliment of warm spices. The secret to making this North Indian-style bread is to roll the dough paper-thin. Lots of elbow grease and practice makes perfect! Be sure the oil is hot enough to cook the breads quickly so they won't absorb excess oil. Try making this bread with baked pumpkin or squash. Experiment with the spices, changing them if you like. For a new twist on a favorite combination of traditional flavors, serve the yam crisps with Turkey Kebabs in Creamed Spinach, page 92, and Oven-Baked Cranberry-Cardamon Chutney, page 127.

1/3 cup peanuts
1/4 cup whole-wheat pastry flour
1 cup all-purpose flour
1/2 cup cooked mashed yam or sweet potato
2 tablespoons plain yogurt
2 tablespoons vegetable oil
1 teaspoon fresh ginger juice
1/2 teaspoon salt
1/4 teaspoon ground cinnamon
1/2 teaspoon ground mace
1/8 teaspoon ground cloves
Few drops water, if needed
Additional all-purpose flour
Vegetable oil for deep-frying

In a blender or food processor fitted with the steel blade, grind peanuts until finely chopped, just before they turn to paste. Sift flours into a small bowl. In a medium-size bowl, combine yam, yogurt, 2 tablespoons oil, ginger juice, salt and spices. With hands, work flours into yam mixture until it forms a medium-firm dough. If needed, add enough water to bind mixture in a dough.

On a lightly floured surface, knead dough 5 minutes or until smooth. Or knead dough 1 minute in a food processor fitted with the steel blade. Shape dough in a 12-inch-long sausage-shaped roll. Cut roll in half; cut each half in 6 pieces. Dip pieces into additional flour; press in flattened round disks. Cover with a kitchen towel to prevent drying. Roll out 1 disk in a circle, 5-inches in diameter, using flour as needed to prevent sticking. Sprinkle with 1 teaspoon of peanuts. Roll dough in a thin cylinder. Holding 1 end of dough, coil cylinder around secured end. Pinch loose end into dough; press and flatten coiled dough-cylinder. Repeat with remaining dough and peanuts. Using a thin Chinese-style rolling pin, roll flattened cylinders in 7- to 8-inch paper-thin circles. Dust lightly with flour. Overlap groups of 2 to 3 circles while rolling remaining cylinders.

In a wok or shallow heavy saucepan, heat oil for deep-frying to 380F (195C) or until a 1-inch cube of bread turns golden-brown in 40 seconds. Slip in 1 circle of dough at a time. Fry about 30 seconds, tapping gently on dough with back of a wooden spoon. This helps steam to form inside dough, causing slight puffing. Turn dough; continue frying 2 to 3 minutes or until lightly colored and very crispy. Drain on paper towels. Repeat with remaining circles of dough. Serve immediately. Makes 12 breads.

HINT
Yam breads stay crispy several hours. Recrisp in a preheated oven 250F (120C) about 5 minutes. Watch carefully; breads burn easily.

LIGHT MEALS

When you mention meat to a Chinese cook, he automatically assumes you mean pork because it is the most common meat eaten in China. When pigs are slaughtered, usually before the Chinese New Year, the meat is salted for long keeping or turned into sausages or fresh ham.

Korean gastronomy was influenced by the neighboring Mongolian nation. As a result they also enjoy eating a diet high in beef. Be sure and try the Spicy Beef Forcemeat Wrapped in Lettuce Leaves, page 103.

The barnyard fowl, content with the low-pecking order in life which compells it to dine upon grains of corn and farmyard scraps, is in reality a culinary star, turning up internationally in the best of kitchens. But no where has the chicken been more warmly welcomed than in the humble kitchens of Asia. From earliest recorded times, Asian cooks have viewed the chicken with high regard. Through the history of Asia, chicken has been a luxury food, prepared as often as economically possible, but usually reserved for special guests and festive occasions.

Moist, tender dark chicken thigh meat has always been an Asian favorite and can withstand a longer cooking period. The Indian recipe for Lesley's Goan Coconut-Chicken Curry, page 99, shows off chicken thighs to their best advantage. This dish is boldly seasoned with distinctive blends of ground spices, herbs and chili peppers.

Fresh fish and seafood are at the heart of the Asian diet. Few cultures understand and appreciate the delicacy of fish cookery so well. The abundance of fish of every kind is well-matched by the unlimited imagination of methods of preparation and the artistic style in which they are always served. Asian cooks insist upon the freshest ingredients in fish cookery. Most prefer to cook fish whole. Fish and seafood are grilled, simmered and deep-fried. They are steamed, dried, pickled, stewed, mashed into nutritious fermented seasoning pastes and enevitably, sliced up with ultimate skill in their natural state and served raw. Squid is a delicious seafood you may not be completely familiar with. It has a fresh mild flavor with a unique, slightly firm texture.

Whatever dish you choose from this chapter to prepare for a light meal, enjoy the magnificient melding of flavors from Asia's rich cuisines.

*Enjoy **Caramelized Lemon Shrimp**, a delicious dish of stir-fried fresh shrimp coated with a rich-tasting caramel syrup and lightly sauced in a spicy, tangy lemon glaze.*

Caramelized Lemon Shrimp   *Viet Nam*

Serve as a light meal or omit the pine nuts and serve with small picks as an appetizer course.

       1 tablespoon white cider vinegar
       3 tablespoons water
       1 teaspoon Southeast Asian fish sauce (nampla)
       1 teaspoon cornstarch
       1/8 teaspoon salt
       1 tablespoon fresh lemon juice
       1 teaspoon Vietnamese-style hot chili sauce
       1 stalk fresh lemongrass or 1/2 teaspoon freshly grated lemon peel
       3 tablespoons vegetable oil
       2 green onions, finely minced
       1 large clove garlic, finely minced
       1 pound fresh large shrimp, peeled, deveined
       3 tablespoons Thin Caramel Syrup, page 27
       1 green onion stem, chopped
       Fresh cilantro leaves
       2 tablespoons toasted pine nuts, if desired

In a small bowl, combine vinegar, water, fish sauce, cornstarch, salt, lemon juice and chili sauce. Mix well to blend cornstarch. If using lemongrass, remove tough outer stalks. Smash inner stalks, thinly slice and mince finely. In a wok or heavy skillet, heat oil over high heat until hot. Stir-fry lemongrass or lemon peel, minced green onions and garlic 10 seconds; add shrimp. Stir-fry 2 to 3 minutes or until shrimp turn pink. Add Thin Caramel Syrup; continue cooking 30 seconds. Reduce heat to medium. Restir cornstarch mixture; pour into shrimp. Cook 1 minute or until shrimp are glazed. Scrape shrimp and glaze onto a heated serving platter. Garnish with green onion stem, cilantro and nuts, if desired. Serve at once. Makes 4 to 6 servings.

Filipino Stir-Fried Shrimp & Pancit Canton

Philippines

"Pancit canton" is a type of dried wheat noodle of Chinese origin, partially precooked, dried and packaged into large, loose bundles. They are readily available in Asian markets and many supermarkets. "Pancit" is the Filipino word for noodle, representing a wide variety of popular noodles such as "pancit Bihon" (thin rice vermicelli) and "pancit Sotanghon" (thin bean threads). Noodle dishes, as well as other Filipino dishes, have evolved through Chinese, Spanish, Creole, Malaysian and American influences. Vary the protein addition in this dish. Try substituting cinnamon-scented roast duck, Cinnamon-Scented Roast Duck Salad in Egg-Flour Wrappers, pages 64-65, Honey Roast Pork, page 108, chicken livers or Chinese sausages.

2 tablespoons dry white wine
1/2 pound raw medium-size shrimp, peeled, deveined
1 teaspoon salt
1 (8-oz.) package dried Philippine-style wheat noodles (pancit canton)
1/4 cup plus 2 tablespoons vegetable oil
1 medium-size onion, chopped
2 large garlic cloves, finely minced
2 teaspoons finely minced fresh gingerroot
2 cups tender green cabbage leaves, cut in 1-inch pieces
1/2 medium-size carrot, thinly sliced, cut in julienne strips
2 tablespoons medium Japanese soy sauce
Several dashes black pepper
2 green onions, thinly sliced
1 tablespoon Southeast Asian fish sauce (patis)
Salt to taste

In a medium-size bowl, sprinkle wine over shrimp. Let stand 10 minutes; drain well. In a large pot, bring 3 quarts water and 1 teaspoon salt to a boil over high heat, add noodles. Cook 3 to 4 minutes or until al dente. Drain noodles in a colander. Stir in 1 tablespoon of oil. Heat a wok or large skillet over high heat. Add 2 tablespoons of oil. When oil is almost to smoking point, add shrimp. Stir-fry 1 minute, just until shrimp turn pink. Remove shrimp.

Wipe wok until clean and dry. Reheat wok; add 2 tablespoons of oil. When oil is hot, add onion, garlic and gingerroot; stir-fry 1 minute. Add cabbage; stir-fry 2 minutes. Add carrot; continue stir-frying 1 minute or until vegetables are crisp-tender. Add remaining oil to wok, if needed. Reduce heat, mix in noodles and shrimp with juices. Season with soy sauce, black pepper, green onions, fish sauce and salt; mix well. Serve at once. Makes 4 to 6 servings.

HINT
This dish can be prepared up to 2 hours ahead. Gently reheat in a wok over low heat until hot.

Chilied Soft-Shell Crabs   *Malaysia*

Atlantic and Gulf blue crabs periodically molt or discard their hard outer shells to grow larger ones. During this period they are called soft-shell crabs. Cleaned soft-shell crabs are especially delicious cooked in this flavorful, spicy-hot tomato sauce. Every delicious bite of the crab can be savored, including the soft outer shell. Most markets will clean soft-shell crabs for you; bring them home for immediate use. If soft-shell crabs are not in season, try this recipe with one pound of fresh jumbo shrimp.

5 to 6 fresh or frozen small soft-shell crabs, thawed, cleaned
3 tablespoons vegetable oil
2 shallots, finely minced
3 garlic cloves, finely minced
1 teaspoon finely minced fresh gingerroot
1 teaspoon cornstarch
1 tablespoon water
1 green onion, finely minced

Chili Sauce:
3 tablespoons tomato sauce
1 tablepoon Indonesian Soy Sauce, page 24, or medium Japanese soy sauce
1 tablespoon ground fresh chili paste (sambal oelek)
1 tablespoon dry white wine
2 tablespoons white cider vinegar
2 tablespoons sugar
1/8 teaspoon salt
1/2 teaspoon sesame seed oil

Prepare Chili Sauce. Rinse crabs. Pat dry with paper towels. Leave whole or cut in half. In a wok or large skillet, heat oil over medium heat until hot. Stir-fry shallots, garlic and gingerroot 2 to 3 minutes or until soft. Increase heat; add crabs. Stir-fry 1 to 2 minutes. Add Chili Sauce; mix with crabs. Reduce heat to medium. Cover and cook 2 to 3 minutes. Combine cornstarch and water in a small dish. Stir into crabs and cook until sauce is slightly thickened. Pour crabs and sauce onto a large serving platter. Garnish with green onion. Serve at once. Makes 3 to 4 servings.

Chili Sauce:
In a small bowl, combine all ingredients. Makes 1/2 cup sauce.

Treat chili peppers with respect when preparing them for cooking. If the volatile oils seem especially irritating, wear kitchen gloves. Contact lens wearers should be especially careful about coming in contact with hot chili oils. Do not touch your eyes or remove contacts with any trace of the oils on your hands. Wash hands thoroughly, even 2 or 3 times, with soap and water after preparing chilies.

Perfumed Basmati Rice Swirled with Saffron & Rose Water

India

Cooked Pullao-style, Northern Indian basmati long-grain rice becomes one of the most splendid rice dishes in the world. A specialty of the Punjabis, this lovely dish with Persian antecedents was created by chefs of Moghul emperors. Considered the prince of rice, aromatic basmati is sautéed in fragrant hot oil before liquid is added. This step helps keep the grains separate while cooking. A mixture of precious saffron-water and perfumed rose water are swirled through a small portion of the white rice and left undisturbed during cooking. The finished dish is a beautiful composition of white and golden grains, studded with whole almonds and golden raisins. Crunchy sweet fried onions adorn the top. If you can't find basmati rice and saffron, make this dish with regular long-grain rice tinted with water colored by an equal amount of musky tumeric, achiote or one-fourth teaspoon yellow food coloring. This dish is wonderful with Indian, Pakistani, Indonesian or Malaysian foods.

> **2 cups plus 1 tablespoon water**
> **1/8 teaspoon crushed saffron threads**
> **1 teaspoon rose water, if desired**
> **2 cups basmati long-grain rice**
> **1/4 cup Ghee, page 25, or 3 tablespoons vegetable oil and 2 tablespoons**
>   **unsalted butter**
> **1 medium-size onion, cut in paper-thin slices**
> **1/4 heaping teaspoon cumin seeds**
> **4 to 5 cardamon pods**
> **2 whole cloves**
> **1 (1-1/2-inch) cinnamon stick**
> **1/3 cup whole blanched almonds**
> **1/3 cup golden raisins**
> **1-1/2 cups chicken stock, Light Coconut Milk, page 21, or water**
> **Juice 1/2 lime or lemon**
> **1 teaspoon salt**
> **1 recipe Crispy Fried Onions, page 26**

In a small bowl, mix 1 tablespoon of water, saffron threads and rose water, if desired. Cover and set aside. Rinse rice as instructed, Basic Cooked White Rice, page 22. Soak rice in 2 cups of water 30 minutes. Drain well; reserve soaking water. In a medium-size saucepan, heat Ghee over medium heat. Add onion; cook 2 minutes or until soft. Add cumin seeds, cardamon pods, cloves and cinnamon stick; continue frying 1 minute more. Add rice. Fry, stirring constantly, 1 to 2 minutes or until grains turn white and become opaque. Stir in almonds and raisins. Add reserved soaking water, chicken stock, lime juice and salt.

When liquid comes to a boil, reduce heat to lowest setting. Cover tightly and cook 12 to 15 minutes. When rice has absorbed liquid but is not yet tender, pour saffron water in a swirl through rice; do not stir. Re-cover and continue cooking 5 to 10 minutes more or until tender. Remove from burner. Let rice stand, covered and undisturbed, 10 minutes. Spoon rice into an attractive serving dish; garnish with Crispy Fried Onions. Serve at once. Makes 6 servings.

VARIATION
Mix 1 cup frozen baby green peas, thawed, with rice 5 minutes before it is done.

Turkey Kebabs in Creamed Spinach   *India*

This wonderful recipe came from Reeva Singh, a native of Dehli, India. While living in America, she experimented and found that ground turkey was an excellent, inexpensive substitute for ground lamb in preparing sautéed kebabs or Indian meat patties. Reeva suggests using half light meat and half dark for moist, juicy kebabs. After sautéing the kebabs, Reeva heats them in a saucepan with several packages of her favorite brand of thawed frozen creamed spinach. I like to place the sautéed kebabs in a serving dish and spread the heated spinach on top with a mustard seed topping. Reeva's kebabs are so easy and taste divine! For effortless entertaining, keep a batch of sautéed kebabs in the freezer. Put them into a baking dish with blocks of frozen creamed spinach on top. The only thing left to do is pop them into the oven for baking until hot.

2 pounds ground turkey, 1/2 white meat and 1/2 dark meat, or ground lamb
2 small fresh whole green chili peppers, stemmed, seeded, finely minced
2 teaspoons finely minced fresh gingerroot
1 medium-size onion, finely minced
2 large garlic cloves, finely minced
1/4 teaspoon ground cinnamon
1/2 teaspoon ground cumin
1/2 teaspoon black pepper
1-1/2 teaspoons salt
2 large eggs
1/4 to 1/2 cup bread crumbs, as needed
1/4 cup vegetable oil
2 (9-oz.) packages frozen creamed spinach, thawed
1 tablespoon vegetable oil, if desired
2 teaspoons black mustard seeds, if desired

In a large bowl, break up ground turkey. Mix in chili peppers, gingerroot, onion, garlic, cinnamon, cumin, black pepper, salt and eggs. Stir in 1/4 cup of bread crumbs. Thawed frozen ground turkey may contain extra moisture requiring additional bread crumbs to form meatballs; add more bread crumbs, if needed.

Shape mixture in 36 to 40 round balls, using 1 generous tablespoon of mixture per kebab. Gently pat each ball in a slightly flattened shape or kebab. In a large skillet, heat 2 tablespoons of oil over medium-high heat. Sauté 1/2 of kebabs on both sides until lightly browned, about 4 to 6 minutes. Drain kebabs. Add 2 tablespoons of oil; repeat with remaining kebabs. Prepare spinach according to package directions. Place kebabs in a single layer in a medium-size shallow casserole dish. Cover with hot spinach.

Serve at once or keep warm in a preheated oven 300F (150C). If desired, to prepare mustard seed topping, heat 1 tablespoon oil in a small skillet over high heat until hot. Add mustard seeds; stir until they pop. Use a lid or a mesh splatter-cover to prevent splattering. Pour hot oil and seeds on top of spinach and meatballs. Serve at once. Makes 6 servings.

Gado Gado, pages 94-95

Gado Gado

This beautifully composed salad features an arrangement of steamed or blanched fresh vegetables accompanied by delicious Peanut Dressing. The shrimp paste in the dressing doesn't have a fishy taste and adds a flavorful dimension, but can be omitted. Tamarind water adds a tart, refreshing taste and rich brown color. If you can't locate it, substitute fresh lemon or lime juice to taste. This dish is always included in the Indonesian "rijsttafel," a banquet-like meal devised by wealthy colonial Dutch settlers. The meal is represented by some of some of the finest dishes throughout the Indonesian archipelago. The "rijsttafel," meaning rice table in Dutch, could be considered a celebration of rice. Early Dutch rice-tables featured magnificent rice dishes, ceremoniously surrounded by dozens of side dishes. The "rijsttafel" is rarely to be found on the tables of most people in Indonesia today. But the concept lives on, usually in modified version, as a unique dining experience in Holland and throughout the world. (Photo on page 93.)

1/2 pound fresh bean sprouts
Fresh banana, ti or cabbage leaves or leaf lettuce
1/2 pound small fresh green beans, trimmed, steamed until crisp-tender,
   cut in half
6 small new potatoes, scrubbed, steamed, cut in wedges
1-1/2 to 2 cups cauliflower florets, steamed until crisp-tender
1/2 small head red cabbage, steamed until crisp-tender, shredded
2 bags cocktail carrots, scrubbed, steamed until crisp-tender
1/2 pound fresh spinach leaves, if desired, dipped into boiling water, chilled in
   iced water, drained
10 to 12 miniature yellow squash or 4 small squash, sliced diagonally
3 hard-cooked eggs, quartered, or 6 hard-cooked quail eggs
1 medium-size red bell pepper, ends trimmed, seeded, ribs removed, cut in
   1/2-inch-wide strips
1 recipe Tofu Nuggets, Crispy-Fried Tofu Nuggets with Condiments, page 68
1 cup fresh cilantro leaves

Crispy Toppings:
1/2 cup finely chopped Five-Spice Nuts, page 129, or peanuts
1 recipe Crispy Fried Shallots, page 26
1 recipe Crispy Fried Garlic, page 26
1 recipe Deep-Fried Shrimp Chips, page 71

Peanut Dressing:
1 stalk fresh lemongrass or 1 teaspoon freshly grated lemon peel
2 tablespoons vegetable oil
2 shallots, minced
1 teaspoon finely minced fresh gingerroot
2 large garlic cloves, finely minced
1 to 2 small fresh whole red chili peppers, stemmed, seeded, ribs
   removed, minced
1/2 teaspoon fermented shrimp paste (trasi or blachan), if desired
1/3 cup homemade peanut butter or other top-quality peanut butter
   without additives

1 cup Light Coconut Milk, page 21, more as needed
1 tablespoon Indonesian Soy Sauce, page 24, or medium Japanese soy sauce
1 teaspoon sesame seed oil
2 tablespoon brown sugar
1/2 teaspoon tamarind concentrate mixed with 1 tablespoon water
Salt and black pepper to taste
2 teaspoons chopped red bell pepper, if desired
Whole chives, if desired

Prepare Crispy Toppings and Peanut Dressing. Pour boiling water over bean sprouts in a colander. Immediately plunge sprouts into iced water. When chilled, drain well. Spread on a kitchen towel or paper towels to absorb excess moisture. Pat gently until dry. To brighten color of banana leaves, dip into boiling water; remove at once. Dip into iced water to chill. Cover a large platter or flat basket with leaves. Arrange remaining salad ingredients in a pleasing design on leaves. Place Peanut Dressing in center. Invite guests to select salad ingredients. Spoon dressing over each serving; garnish with Crispy Toppings. Makes 6 to 8 servings.

Crispy Toppings:
Serve each topping separately in a small bowl.

Peanut Dressing:
If using lemongrass, remove tough outer stalk. Smash inner stalk, thinly slice and mince finely. In a wok or medium-size skillet, heat oil over medium heat until hot. Add lemongrass or lemon peel, shallots, gingerroot, garlic, chili peppers and shrimp paste, if desired. Stir-fry 4 or 5 minutes or until aromatic and tender. Do not allow ingredients to burn. Blend in peanut butter until melted. Remove from heat.

In a blender or food processor fitted with the steel blade, process peanut mixture to form a paste as smooth as possible. With machine running, pour in Light Coconut Milk, a little at a time. Scrape down sides of container 1 or 2 times. Pour mixture back into wok. Add Indonesian Soy Sauce, sesame seed oil, brown sugar and tamarind water. Stir and cook mixture 10 minutes over medium-low heat. Add salt and pepper. Thin dressing with additional coconut milk, if desired. Serve at once or cover and refrigerate. Bring back to room temperature before serving. Garnish with bell pepper and chives, if desired. Makes about 1-1/2 cups.

HINT
Salad is best served at room temperature. Ingredients can be held at room temperature for a short time. If refrigerated, bring to room temperature before serving.

*To prepare **Cannery Row Glazed Squid Blossoms**, clean the squid and wipe clean with damp paper towels.*

Combine stir-fried marinated squid and vegetables with Oyster Sauce Glaze and serve hot.

Choose the correct soy sauce for the intended use. The flavors and taste of saltier Chinese soy sauce are not compatible with the delicate flavors of Japanese cooking. Light or thin soy sauce is saltier than medium dark soy sauce. Look for "sheng cho" or light Chinese soy sauce and use "usukuchi shoyu" or light Japanese soy sauce. Medium darker-colored soy sauce is a good all-purpose soy sauce for cooking and for the table. Dark mushroom-flavored Chinese soy sauce is available in Asian markets. If you cannot locate Chinese soy sauce, use top-quality Japanese soy sauce such as the types make by Kikkoman.

Cannery Row Glazed Squid Blossoms

Squid is a cephalopod from the mollusk family with a mild sweet taste and a slightly firm texture similar to abalone. The secrets for preparing squid have been shared in Lillian Johnson's recipe, passed from her mother Frances Yee who learned them from grandfather Yee Won from Canton, China. In the early 1900's, Yee brought new life to California's Monterey Peninsula when he perfected drying techniques and invented an important machine for baling and compressing dried squid for export to Hong Kong and China. His small squid shop, Wing Chong ("glorious, successful"), on Ocean View Avenue, is now a landmark in Cannery Row. Yee Won and his squid shop were immortalized by John Steinbeck in his famous novel, *Cannery Row*.

8 small dried shiitake mushrooms
1-1/2 to 2 pounds fresh small squid or 1 pound squid steaks
2 teaspoons grated fresh gingerroot
2 garlic cloves, minced
1 teaspoon hoisin sauce
1-1/2 tablespoons light Chinese soy sauce
2 tablespoons bourbon or gin
5 tablespoons vegetable oil
1 medium-size onion, cut in half, thinly sliced
2 stalks celery, thinly sliced diagonally
1 small red bell pepper, ends trimmed, seeded, ribs removed, cut in cubes
1/4 pound fresh Chinese pea pods, blanched, chilled in iced water, drained
1/2 (1-lb.) can miniature ears baby corn, well-rinsed
2 tablespoons chopped Szechuan preserved vegetable (kohlrabi) or 1 teaspoon
   chili paste with garlic, if desired

Oyster Sauce Glaze:
1 to 2 teaspoons cornstarch
2 to 3 tablespoons water, bourbon or gin
1-1/2 teaspoons oyster sauce

In a medium-size bowl, cover mushrooms with warm water. Soak 30 minutes or until needed. Squeeze mushrooms dry. Cut off and discard tough stems. Leave small mushrooms whole or cut in half.

To clean squid, firmly grasp tentacles with 1 hand and mantle (body) with other hand. With a firm pull, remove tentacles and most of viscera from body. Slit squid open lengthwise. Pull out quill-like cartlidge. With back of a knife, scrape out remaining viscera. Peel off thin outer skin. Do not rinse squid. Wipe clean with damp paper towels. Rinsed squid absorbs water like a sponge.

Score inside of squid with crisscross diagonal slices; seasonings will penetrate squid more readily and make it easier to eat. Cut each squid in quarters. If using squid steak, score and cut in smaller pieces.

In a medium-size bowl, combine 1 teaspoon of gingerroot, hoisin sauce, soy sauce and bourbon. Add squid; let stand 10 minutes to 1 hour. Prepare Oyster Sauce Glaze. Heat a wok or large skillet over high heat. Add 3 tablespoons of oil. When hot, stir-fry squid quickly, no more than 1 to 2 minutes. Remove to a platter. Reheat wok; add remaining oil. When hot, add mushrooms, remaining gingerroot, garlic, onion, celery and bell pepper; stir-fry 1 to 2 minutes. Add pea pods, corn and preserved vegetable, if desired. When hot, return squid to wok. Restir Oyster Sauce Glaze; pour into wok. Stir-fry 1 minute or just until glaze is thickened. Pour into a serving dish. Serve at once. Makes 4 servings.

Oyster Sauce Glaze:
In a small bowl, combine all ingredients. Make about 2 tablespoons.

Thousand Year Sauce Chicken   *China*

Long ago in China, a treasured crock of "master sauce" was sometimes included in the trousseau of a new bride. Used for "red cooking" or braising meats and poultry, the sauce was strained after use and stored in a cool place for reuse. Basic ingredients were periodically added to perpetuate the supply. Some brides claimed their secret sauce had been passed down through generations. Perhaps it was treasured as a talisman, a charm to bring marital good fortune and to assure success in perputating the family lineage. This in turn would insure that family worship for the good health of the ancestral spirits would continue, perhaps for a thousand years! I cannot promise you'll be making the elixir of immortality, but I will promise a rich-tasting, delicious sauce which will guarantee the applause and approval of all mere mortals. Prepare tasty appetizers by simmering hard-cooked eggs and chicken livers in the sauce until they become coated and a rich mahogany color. Serve sauce over Basic Cooked White Rice, page 22, or cooked noodles.

> **1 (3- to 3-1/2 lb.) broiler-fryer**
> **Small amount water, if necessary**
> **10 to 12 green onions, smashed, slivered in 2-inch pieces.**
>
> *Fragrant Master Sauce:*
> **2/3 cup medium Chinese or Japanese soy sauce**
> **2 cups water**
> **2 tablespoons dry white wine**
> **3 (1/8-inch-thick) slices fresh gingerroot, smashed**
> **1/2 cup sugar**
> **2 whole star anise**
> **1 green onion, cut in half**

Prepare Fragrant Master Sauce. Add chicken to sauce; bring sauce to a boil. Reduce heat and partially cover. Cook 30 minutes, turning chicken often for even glazing. Continue cooking and turning chicken until it is a rich mahogany color and tender. Sauce should be considerably reduced and slightly glazed. If sauce is too rich, thin with a small amount of water. Cool chicken slightly before carving in serving size pieces. On a large serving platter, arrange chicken pieces. Sprinkle green onions around base of chicken. Spoon warm sauce over chicken just before serving. Refrigerate leftover chicken; enjoy cold or reheat. Makes 4 to 6 servings.

Fragrant Master Sauce:
In a wok or medium-size deep saucepan, combine all ingredients. Simmer over medium heat 2 to 3 minutes to dissolve sugar. Makes about 2 cups sauce.

VARIATION
Substitute 3 to 4 pounds of chicken-wing drumsticks for broiler-fryer. Serve as a snack or appetizer. Keep warm in a chafing dish, electric wok or crockpot. Makes 6 servings.

Lesley's Goan Coconut-Chicken Curry   *India*

My British friend Lesley van der Schroeff spent years working as an air hostess in Bahrain in the Arabian Gulf. Regular hops to Bombay provided her with ample time to explore the country and learn about Indian cuisine. Her exquisitely-spiced coconut curry can be made and refrigerated one day before serving. Chicken bones enrich the curry sauce; remove them from the chicken pieces before heating and serving the curry. Long, slow cooking reduces the onion mixture to a paste, which acts as the thickening agent. Commercially prepared curry powder, as we know it, does not exist in India. Instead of a single "catch-all" spice-blend for cooking, Indian cooks imaginatively combine spices and herbs in hundreds of fascinating ways. Lesley always grinds her own spices to make a "masala" (seasoning blend). For the best flavor, be sure and use the freshest spices you can buy.

 1/4 cup fresh lemon juice
 3 to 3-1/2 pounds chicken thighs
 1/3 cup Ghee, page 25, or 3 tablespoons vegetable oil and 2 tablespoons
   unsalted butter
 2 large sweet white onions, thinly sliced
 4 large garlic cloves, finely minced
 1 (2-inch) cinnamon stick, broken in small pieces
 8 whole cloves
 8 cardamon pods
 1 tablespoon coriander seeds or 1 teaspoon ground coriander
 1 tablespoon ground tumeric
 1 teaspoon black pepper
 2 small fresh whole green or red chili peppers, stemmed, seeded, sliced lengthwise
 Small amount water, if needed
 4 cups Light Coconut Milk, page 21, or 3 cups canned coconut milk diluted with
   1 cup water
 1 teaspoon salt or to taste

In a medium-size bowl, pour lemon juice over chicken. Let stand 30 minutes. In a heavy saucepan, heat Ghee over medium-low heat. Add onions and garlic. Fry, stirring occasionally, 15 minutes or until onions are very soft. In a small skillet, stir and toast cinnamon over medium heat. Add cloves, cardamon pods and coriander seeds; stir until spices are aromatic. In a small electric coffee mill, grind spices to a powder. Stir ground spices, tumeric and black pepper into onions and garlic. Add chili peppers.

 Cook slowly, stirring often, 15 minutes or until onions begin to lose their shape. If mixture is cooking too fast, reduce heat or add a small amount of water. Oil will begin to separate from mixture and come to top. Add chicken; coat well with onion mixture. Fry 1 to 2 minutes. Add 2 cups of Light Coconut Milk. Cover and simmer 20 minutes. Add remaining coconut milk. Simmer, uncovered, 20 minutes more. Add salt. Makes 8 servings.

VARIATION
Substitute 2-1/2 to 3 pounds cubed beef pot roast for chicken. Simmer until tender.

Pink Rice-Stick Noodles
with Seafood & Vegetables
Thailand

The thin, wiry noodles in this dish are made from flour which has been made from pounded rice. They are wonderfully absorbent, soaking up the seasonings and flavors of the foods with which they are cooked. Sometimes called rice-sticks or rice vermicelli, the soaked noodles will naturally break in shorter lengths as they are cooked, eliminating the precutting necessary for tougher bean thread noodles. If you would like to enjoy the pleasant taste and texture of plain rice sticks, simmer them in water two to three minutes after soaking. When deep-fried, unsoaked rice-sticks dramatically puff up into a mass resembling a bird's nest. Follow the directions for making Crispy Fried Rice Sticks, Shredded Beef & Almonds in Lettuce Cups, pages 36-37.

2 tablespoons Southeast Asian fish sauce (nampla) or as needed
1/4 cup ketchup
1 tablespoon sugar
1/4 teaspoon black pepper
1/3 cup plus 2 tablespoons vegetable oil
1 small green bell pepper, ends trimmed, seeded, ribs removed, cut in
    julienne strips
1/2 large carrot, cut in julienne strips
1 to 2 small fresh whole red chili peppers, stemmed, seeded, minced,
2 cups fresh bean sprouts
6 to 8 shallots, thinly sliced
3 large garlic cloves, finely minced
2 teaspoons finely minced fresh gingerroot
3/4 pound raw medium-size shrimp, peeled, deveined
1/2 pound sea scallops, cut in half horizontally or 1/2 pound cleaned small squid,
    cut in 1/2-inch rings
6 ounces thin rice-stick noodles, soaked in warm water 30 minutes, well-drained
2 large eggs, softly scrambled
3 small green onions, thinly sliced
Salt to taste, if desired
1/4 cup chopped peanuts
1/2 bunch fresh cilantro leaves
1 green onion stem, chopped
1 lime, cut in thin slices

To prepare sauce, in a small bowl, combine fish sauce, ketchup, sugar and black pepper. In a wok or large skillet, heat 2 tablespoons of oil over high heat until hot. Stir-fry bell pepper, carrot and chili pepper 1 to 2 minutes. Add bean sprouts; cook 1 minute more. Remove vegetables. Wipe wok dry with paper towels. Reheat wok or skillet over high heat. Add remaining oil. Stir-fry shallots until soft; add garlic and gingerroot. Cook 1 minute more. Add shrimp and scallops. Stir fry 2 to 3 minutes or until shrimp are pink and scallops are white and barely firm.

  Reduce heat to medium-low. Add vegetables and noodles to seafood; carefully blend ingredients. Pour sauce over noodles; continue blending until noodles are coated and turn pink. Blend in eggs and green onions. Add additional fish sauce or salt, if desired. Remove noodles to a serving platter. Garnish with peanuts, cilantro, green onion stem and lime. Serve at once. Makes 6 to 8 servings.

Pink Rice-Stick Noodles with Seafood & Vegetables

Lu Chu Pot Roast Noodles

Okinawa

Okinawa is the largest of the Ryukyuan Islands, the Japanese island chain located about 400 miles south of Kyushu. Lu Chu is the old Chinese name for the Ryukyuan Islands, under Chinese rule for several centuries. Although now part of Japan, the islanders enjoy a rich, separate culture, producing some of the finest textiles, lacquerware and folkcrafts in the world. Their exquisite folk pottery helped inspire the birth of Japan's folkcraft movement. Their cuisine is a unique blending of Japanese foodstuffs, often prepared with Chinese cooking methods. Like the Chinese, Okinawans consider pork their favorite meat; both cultures enjoy eating Chinese-style noodles. The hearty braised pork has Chinese overtones. It is sliced and served over noodles like Japanese "domburi," a meal in a bowl. The sea vegetable "konbu" is a natural and healthful source of amino acids used in the manufacturer of monosodium glutimate. It serves to enhance the rich flavors of the delicious sauce.

1 tablespon vegetable oil
1 (3-1/2- to 4-lb.) boneless pork shoulder roast, tied
2 green onions, cut in half
1 (1/4-inch-thick) slice fresh gingerroot, smashed
2 large garlic cloves, smashed
6 cups Gingery Chicken Stock, page 26
1 (5-inch) square dashi konbu
1/4 cup red miso
2 to 4 tablespoons medium Japanese soy sauce
1 pound Chinese egg noodles, cooked al dente
1 pound fresh spinach, trimmed, rinsed, blanched 30 seconds

In a large saucepan, heat oil until hot. Sauté pork until browned. Add onions, gingerroot and garlic; sauté 1 minute. Add Gingery Chicken Stock. When stock boils, reduce heat. With a damp cloth, wipe konbu lightly. Cook in stock 3 to 5 minutes until softened. Remove from stock. With kitchen scissors, cut konbu in 5 strips. Tie a knot in middle of each strip. Drop knotted strips into stock.

Partially cover and simmer 1-1/2 to 2 hours or until pork is tender. Stir in miso and soy sauce; simmer 15 minutes. Remove pork; cut off strings. Slice pork in small pieces. Divide noodles among 6 to 8 deep serving bowls. Place slices of pork on top of noodles and a few pieces of spinach in each bowl. Ladle sauce over each serving of pork and noodles. Serve at once. Or cool pork in sauce, cover and refrigerate overnight. Makes 6 to 8 servings.

Spicy Beef Forcemeat
Wrapped in Lettuce Leaves

Korea

The spicy cuisine of the Korean peninsula is as unique and individualistic as its people. Flavorful red peppers accent Korean foods and are available fresh, dried, ground and shredded in dried threadlike strings. "Kochu jang" is a cinnabar-colored, fermented red pepper paste often used in preparing soups, stews and beef dishes. Slightly softer than Japanese miso paste, the flavor of this velvety-smooth condiment could become addictive! You will love its distinctive taste in the Spicy Beef Forcemeat.

Boston lettuce leaves
1/2 cup pine nuts
1 recipe Basic Cooked White Rice (short-grain), page 22

Spicy Beef Forcemeat:
2 tablespoons vegetable oil
2 large garlic cloves, finely minced
2 small onions, finely minced
1 tablespoon finely minced fresh gingerroot
1 pound lean ground beef
1/4 cup Korean red-pepper paste (kochu jang)
1 teaspoon medium Japanese soy sauce
1 teaspoon sugar
1/4 teaspoon black pepper
1/2 teaspoon sesame seed oil
1 tablespoon Dry Roasted Sesame Seeds, page 24
2 green onions, finely minced
Salt to taste

Preheat oven to 350F (175C). Separate lettuce leaves, rinse and pat thoroughly dry. Store in a zip-type plastic bag until needed. On a baking sheet, toast nuts, stirring often, in preheated oven 6 to 8 minutes. Watch carefully so they do not burn. Prepare Spicy Beef Forcemeat. Place lettuce leaves on a serving plate. Put nuts, Basic Cooked White Rice and beef mixture into separate serving dishes. Invite guests to stuff and roll their own lettuce leaves. To fill a lettuce leaf, spoon 1 small spoonful each of rice and filling in center of leaf. Sprinkle with a few nuts. Fold up sides of lettuce in a bundle. Makes 6 to 8 servings.

Spicy Beef Forcemeat:
In a wok or large skillet, heat oil over medium heat until hot. Fry garlic, onions and gingerroot 2 to 3 minutes or until soft. Add ground beef; fry, breaking up any large pieces, until no longer pink. Mix in red-pepper paste, soy sauce, sugar, black pepper, sesame seed oil and Dry Roasted Sesame Seeds. Stir in green onions and salt. Serve at once. Or cool, cover and refrigerate overnight. Reheat in a wok on low heat. Makes about 2-1/2 cups.

VARIATION
To prepare *Spicy Beef & Pine Nuts with Noodles*, mix Spicy Beef Forcemeat with 3/4 pound cooked Chinese-style egg noodles. Sprinkle with 1/2 cup toasted pine nuts.

Japanese-Style Pizza
Japan

"Okonomiyaki" (Japanese pizza) is a type of savory pancake made with a flour and egg batter and a multitude of ingredients such as meats, vegetables and seafood. Whatever other ingredients are added, they always include shredded cabbage and "beni shoga" (red pickled ginger). A style of "teppan yaki" cooking (pan-grilled foods), the name "okonomiyaki" indicates that the pizza is cooked "as you like it." In Japan, I enjoyed various forms of "okonomiyaki" in the homes of Japanese friends, from street vendors and in special restaurants where everyone gathered around the griddle-table to create their own. A Japanese-style pizza party is a unique and delightful way to entertain family and friends.

3 cups cake flour
1-3/4 cups water
1/2 teaspoon salt
1 teaspoon baking powder
6 medium-size eggs
3 cups finely shredded cabbage
6 green onions, thinly sliced
Vegetable oil as needed
2 tablespoons shredded red pickled ginger (beni shoga)
Powdered green seaweed (ao-noriko), if desired
Dried bonito thread-shavings, (ito-kezuri-katsuo), if desired
Lemon-Ginger Dressing, page 130, as desired

Okonomiyaki Sauce:
1 cup ketchup
2 tablespoons sugar
1/4 cup soy sauce
2 tablespoons Japanese sweet rice wine (mirin)
1 tablespoon Worcestershire sauce
1 teaspoon finely minced fresh gingerroot
1 large garlic clove, finely minced

Additional Ingredients:
4 to 6 medium-size dried shiitake mushrooms, rehydrated, stemmed, sliced
1 carrot, cut in matchstick julienne strips
1/4 pound bean sprouts
4 ounces cooked thin wheat noodles, coated with soy sauce
Crispy fried bits (age-dama), Shrimp & Onion Fritters, page 80
1/2 pound baked ham, cut in paper-thin slices
1/2 pound boneless pork, cut in 1/8-inch-thick slices
1/2 pound tender beef, cut in 1/8-inch-thick slices
12 strips bacon, cut in small pieces
1/2 pound small squid, cleaned as instructed, Cannery Row Glazed Squid
  Blossoms, page 97, cut in thin strips
1/2 pound raw medium-size shrimp, peeled, deveined, cut in half horizontally

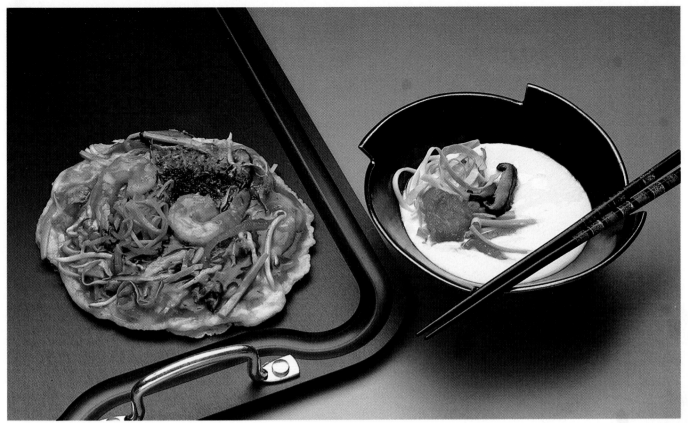

*To prepare savory **Japanese-Style Pizza**, cook the batter with meats, vegetables and seafood on a griddle. Top with Okonomiyaki Sauce and sprinkle with toppings.*

Prepare Okonomiyaki Sauce. In a large bowl, combine cake flour, water, salt and baking powder. Divide batter among 6 medium-size deep bowls. Arrange eggs, cabbage and green onions on table for cooking. Each guest receives a bowl of batter. Stir 1 egg into each bowl of batter. Divide cabbage and green onion among bowls; stir into batter. If desired, stir in small amounts of vegetables, noodles or crispy fried bits from Additional Ingredients.

Heat an electric griddle or an electric frying pan over medium-high heat; add oil. For each pizza place a small pile of 1 type meat or seafood or a combination from Additional Ingredients on griddle. Turn once; grill until almost done. Cover each pile with 1 bowl of batter and vegetables. Cook on 1 side until pizzas are set and lightly brown; flip and cook until done. Remove pizzas to a serving platter. Spread with Okonomiyaki Sauce. Top with pickled ginger, powdered green seaweed and bonito thread shavings, if desired. Add Lemon-Ginger Dressing, as desired. Makes 6 servings.

Okonomiyaki Sauce:
In a medium-size bowl, combine all ingredients. Makes about 1-1/2 cups.

Additional Ingredients:
Select several items from vegetables, noodles or crispy fried bits. Make 2 to 3 meat and seafood selections. Arrange ingredients attractively on a large platter.

HINT
As pizzas are cooked, cut each one in 6 pieces. Guests can sample 6 different combinations.
Serve pizzas with steaming hot cups of green tea, soft drinks or cold beer.

Steamed Egg Buns Stuffed with Honey Roast Pork & Oyster Sauce
China

Tender, plump egg buns are stuffed with diced Honey Roast Pork and a well-seasoned oyster sauce. The distinctive filling complements the mild background flavor of the rich dough. Rolled circles of dough are pleated around the edge to enclose the filling. To duplicate the thin Chinese rolling pin, use a 1-inch in diameter unfinished dowel rod cut 10- to 12-inches long. When you see these Chinese buns with their pleated tops slightly opened from steaming, you will know that, according to tradition, the filling will be a savory one. If the steamed bun is rounded and smooth on top and the pleat is hidden on the bottom, the chances are good the filling might be a sweet one. To stuff the buns with sweet treasures, follow the directions below, but fill them with Pineapple Conserve, Taiwanese Pineapple Wedding Cake, page 145, or Date & Prune Paste, Autumn Moon Cakes, pages 142-143.

2 tablespoons vegetable oil
3 green onions, finely minced
1 large garlic clove, finely minced
1/2 pound Honey Roast Pork, page 108, diced in small pieces
3 tablespoons oyster sauce
1 tablespoon medium Chinese or Japanese soy sauce
1/4 cup chicken stock
1/2 heaping teaspoon cornstarch
1/2 teaspoon sesame seed oil
Dash black pepper
1 tablespoon honey
1 to 2 tablespoons fresh cilantro leaves, torn
1 recipe Rich Egg Dough, page 30

To make filling, heat a wok or small skillet over medium heat. Add oil. When oil is hot, stir-fry green onions and garlic 10 seconds. Add pork; cook 30 seconds. In a small bowl, mix oyster sauce, soy sauce, chicken stock, cornstarch, sesame seed oil, black pepper and honey. Add to pork mixture. Stir-fry until mixture thickens, about 1 minute. Stir in cilantro. Cool completely.

On a lightly floured surface, shape Rich Egg Dough in a 12-inch-long roll. Cut in half; cut each half in 6 pieces. Place pieces of dough, cut sides down, on floured surface. With fingers, flatten each piece slightly in a rounded shape. With a Chinese-style rolling pin, roll out each piece of dough in a 4-inch circle. Chinese rolling method requires use of fingers and palm of 1 hand to push thin rolling pin up to center of dough; do not flatten center. Roll pin back to edge where rolling began. At same time, fingers of other hand will be positioned under top portion of dough circle, turning it counterclockwise upon completion of each full roll. Edges of dough should be thinner than center, which must be strong to support filling.

Spoon 1 tablespoon of filling in center of each dough circle. Enclose filling by pleating edge until opening is closed; pinch tightly. Repeat with remaining filling and dough circles. Cut 12 squares of foil, parchment paper or waxed paper slightly larger than buns. Lightly oil squares. Place 1 bun, pleated-side-up, on each square. Place buns at least 1 inch apart on a steamer tray and cover. Let rise 20 minutes. In a wok or deep pot, bring 6 cups water to a boil. Place tray over boiling water. Steam buns about 15 minutes or until dough is cooked. Remove buns from squares. Cool 5 minutes before cutting. Makes 12 large buns.

HINT
Buns can be prepared ahead and refrigerated in an airtight plastic bag. Reheat in a microwave oven or resteam 3 to 5 minutes.

ORIENTAL BARBECUE

Throughout the period of Asia's recorded history, foods have been cooked over an open fire. Even earlier, we know that the Peking Man in the Plesistocene period dined on game meat cooked with fire. Unlike the methods of leisurely recreational grilling we enjoy today, foods were cooked over fire from necessity rather than as a culinary diversion. Cooking utensils, fuel and foods were often scarce. Even today in many areas of Asia, kitchens and cooking appliances as we know them do not exist. To prepare a meal, the family cook will light a small fire in order to cook the rice, grill the family's modest portion of meat or perhaps combine it with a few vegetables in a wok to be stir-fried. If the fuel supply is plentiful, the fire will stay lit throughout the day.

In Europe and North America, barbecued and grilled foods are enjoying a new renaissance. Barbecuing food refers to covered cooking over charcoal or smoking over low heat for a long period. Grilling means cooking foods more quickly over a hot open fire. Juices from the foods drip into the fire and create smoke which adds flavor to the food. The heat source can be wood, charcoal or even gas. The backyard barbecue grill was popularized in America in the 1950's and 1960's. According to a recent survey by the National Broiler Council, approximately seventy-four percent of this nation's families cook out at least once a week. Americans can be found firing up their grills year-round, even in the dead of winter. They just never give up.

The next time you plan to grill hamburgers, instead try Dee's Spicy Grilled Lamb Pockets, page 124. Pita bread rounds are stuffed with grilled lamb kebabs (patties) and spicy-hot Cucumber-Onion Relish. Poultry is often found on Asian and American grills. Nonya-Style Grilled Lemon Chicken, page 111, is an easy, low calorie Malaysian dish with a "finger-licking good" light and lemony taste.

Smoked turkey is very much an American institution. Seasoned with Chinese spices before cooking, it takes on an exciting and unexpected delicious new appeal. Even as the ancient Chinese Mongols experimented with different woods for smoking, so can you when you prepare Peking-Style Smoked Turkey with Cornmeal Pancakes, page 113. If desired, vary the subtle, smoky downhome flavor of hickory and substitute chips of oak, apple, or cherry, grapevines or a small amount of Southwestern mesquite.

Honey Roast Pork

China

Because home ovens are a scarcity in China, food shops abound which specialize in selling roasted meats and poultry. Succulent, versatile Chinese roast pork can be served as a main course or added to stir-fried vegetable dishes, fried rice or noodle dishes. Use it as a filling ingredient in Chinese filled buns and pastries or make sandwiches of sliced roast pork stuffed into Chinese-Style Steamed Sandwich Buns, page 116. Roast meats are often stained bright red, but the coloring can easily be omitted. Try the Chinese Barbecue Sauce on spareribs, whole pork tenderloins, pork shoulders, steaks, chicken, duck or rock cornish hens.

1 (3-lb.) boneless pork shoulder roast (Boston butt)

Chinese Barbecue Sauce:
3 tablespoons hoisin sauce
2 tablespoons ketchup
1/4 cup medium Chinese or Japanese soy sauce
2 tablespoons dry white wine
1/2 teaspoon five-spice powder
1/8 teaspon ground cinnamon
1 large garlic clove, finely minced
1 teaspoon finely minced fresh gingeroot
1 teaspoon brown sugar
1 teaspoon ground fresh chili paste (sambal oelek) or Vietnamese-style hot
   chili sauce

Honey Glaze:
1/4 cup honey
2 teaspoons sesame seed oil
Red food coloring, if desired

Prepare Chinese Barbecue Sauce. With a large sharp knife, cut pork roast in slices about 1-1/2-inches thick, then in strips about 2-inches wide. Cut strips in half crosswise. Place pork strips in dish of Chinese Barbecue Sauce; coat well. Cover tightly and refrigerate at least 6 hours or up to 24 hours. Remove pork from refrigerator and preheat charcoal grill 30 minutes before cooking. Prepare Honey Glaze. Scrape excess sauce off pork strips. Reserve sauce.

Grill pork, turning and basting often with reserved sauce, over a moderate fire 20 minutes. With a small kitchen brush, paint pork strips with Honey Glaze. Continue turning pork strips and brushing with glaze 15 to 20 minutes. Pork should be crusty and slightly charred on outside and no longer pink inside, yet still juicy. Makes 6 to 8 servings.

Chinese Barbecue Sauce:
In a large nonaluminum baking dish, combine all ingredients. Makes about 2/3 cup.

Honey Glaze:
In a small bowl, combine honey, sesame seed oil and food coloring, if desired. Mixture will become thick. Makes 1/4 cup.

HINT
To roast Honey Roast Pork in oven, hang pork strips on S-shaped hooks from an oven rack raised to highest position. Place a foil-lined pan under meat. Or place pork strips on a rack set inside a foil-lined pan. Roast in a preheated oven 375F (190C) 25 to 30 minutes or until crispy on outside and done inside.

Vietnamese Pork Barbecue Platter   *Viet Nam*

Pork is the preferred meat in Viet Nam, preferably marinated and grilled. In Viet Nam, an aromatic lemon leaf might be wrapped around each pork cube before grilling. The leaves protect the pieces of pork from burning and imbue them with a special fragrance. (Photo of *Skewered Pork* on cover.)

Red or green leaf lettuce
Boston or bibb butterhead lettuce
4 ounces dried rice vermicelli, soaked 30 minutes, simmered 1 to 2
    minutes, drained
12 (6- to 8-inch) round rice paper wrappers, lightly brushed with a pastry brush
    dipped into water
1/2 small red Bermuda onion, cut in thin slices
1 European cucumber, cut in paper-thin ribbon slices
1 large carrot, cut in paper-thin ribbon slices
Fresh cilantro leaves
Fresh sweet basil leaves, purple basil or lemon-scented basil
Unsprayed colorful edible flowers
1 recipe Nuoc Cham Dipping Sauce, page 136

Skewered Pork:
2 stalks fresh lemongrass or 2 teaspoons freshly grated lemon peel
2 large garlic cloves, finely minced
3 tablespoons dry white wine
1 teaspoon salt
1/4 teaspoon black pepper
2 tablespoons honey
2 tablespoons vegetable oil
1 to 2 tablespoons Southeast Asian fish sauce (nampla)
2 green onions, finely minced
About 1-1/2 pounds trimmed boned pork loin, partially frozen
1 package bamboo skewers, 6- to 8-inches long, soaked in cold water
Finely chopped roasted peanuts

Prepare Skewered Pork. Line a platter with red leaf lettuce. Arrange Boston lettuce leaves, vermicelli, rice paper wrappers, onion, cucumber, carrot, cilantro, basil and flowers attractively in separate piles on red leaf lettuce. Arrange Skewered Pork on platter. Invite guests to line rice paper wrappers with Boston lettuce leaves and enclose small portions of pork, vermicelli and garden ingredients in sandwich-like bundles. Serve with Nuoc Cham Dipping Sauce. Makes 6 servings.

Skewered Pork:
To make marinade, if using lemongrass, remove tough outer stalks. Smash inner stalks, thinly slice and mince finely. With a mortar and pestle, grind lemongrass or lemon peel and garlic to a paste. Scrape mixture into a large bowl. Rinse mortar with wine; add to paste. Add salt, black pepper, honey, oil, fish sauce and green onions; mix well.

  Cut pork in cubes, about 3/4-inch square. Add pork cubes to marinade; combine until well coated. Cover and refrigerate at least 4 hours or overnight. Preheat grill 30 minutes. Lace 3 to 4 pork cubes on each bamboo skewer. Grill pork, turning often, 5 to 6 minutes or until no longer pink inside. Sprinkle with peanuts. Makes 12 skewers of pork.

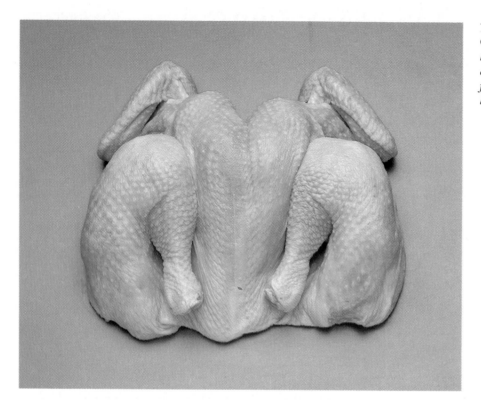

To prepare **Nonya-Style Grilled Lemon Chicken**, *remove the wing tips and the backbone of the chicken. Place the chicken, breast up, on a flat surface and flatten the chicken by breaking the breastbone.*

Grilled Chicken Slices in Red Pepper Paste

Korea

Thinly sliced chicken breasts are soaked in a spicy marinade, then quickly grilled over charcoal. During picnic outings in Korea, marinated chicken and beef slices are sometimes grilled on large flat heated rocks. The chicken tastes fantastic grilled over charcoal, but can be successfully cooked on a portable tabletop grill or griddle. If you own one, grill the chicken on a Ghengis Khan grill pan placed over a portable tabletop burner. The iron dome-shaped pan resembles the ancient Mongolian warrior's protective helmet.

4 chicken breast halves, skinned, boned, partially frozen
2 tablespoons medium Japanese soy sauce
3 green onions, smashed, slivered
2 large garlic cloves, finely minced
1 tablespoon Dry Roasted Sesame Seeds, page 24
3 tablespoons dry white wine
1 tablespoon sugar
2 tablespoons Korean red bean paste (kochu jang)

Preheat hibachi, portable tabletop-grill or griddle. Slice each chicken breast half in 1/8- to 1/4-inch-thick diagonal strips. In a medium-size bowl, combine remaining ingredients. Coat chicken with mixture. Grill chicken, turning several times, 2 to 3 minutes or until done. Recipe can be doubled. Makes 4 servings.

Nonya-Style Grilled Lemon Chicken   *Malaysia*

The fresh lemony flavor comes from the aromatic grass called citronella or lemongrass. Used extensively throughout Southeast Asia, lemongrass is easily grown and should be considered for cultivation in the herb garden. If you find stalks with roots attached, put them in water to increase the root system, then transplant to a large pot of soil. Flattening the chicken for grilling has several advantages. It will cook quicker and more evenly. Left in one piece, the chicken retains valuable juices. This is a great method for preparing rock cornish hens or duck.

> 1 (3- to 3-1/2-lb.) broiler-fryer
> 2 stalks fresh lemongrass or 2 teaspoons freshly grated lemon peel
> 1/2 cup Light Coconut Milk, page 21, or canned coconut milk
> 1/4 teaspoon black pepper
> 1/2 teaspoon salt
> 1 teaspoon ground tumeric
> 1/2 teaspoon finely minced fresh gingerroot
> 2 large garlic cloves, finely minced
> 1 tablespoon Indonesian Soy Sauce, page 24
> 1/8 to 1/4 teaspoon red pepper (cayenne)
> 1/2 teaspoon tamarind concentrate mixed with 2 tablespoons water or 2
>   tablespoons fresh lime or lemon juice

To cut up chicken, remove wing tips with poultry shears or a large sharp knife. Remove backbone by cutting through chicken ribs on either side of backbone from neck to tail. Turn chicken over, breast up. Break breastbone and flatten chicken by firmly striking breast with heel of hand or a heavy kitchen mallet.

If using lemongrass, remove tough outer stalks. Smash inner stalks, thinly slice and mince finely. In a large bowl, combine lemongrass or lemon peel and remaining ingredients. Coat chicken with marinade mixture. Place chicken in a shallow baking dish; pour on marinade. Cover and refrigerate at least 4 hours or overnight. Preheat charcoal grill 30 minutes. Grill chicken, turning several times and basting often with marinade, over moderate heat 25 to 30 minutes or until juices run clear. Makes 4 servings.

The preparation of foods from the Far East allows the cook freedom to be flexible and adaptable. It is equally important not to take too many short cuts and compromise quality. Please do not substitute salty bouillon cubes for a good savory stock and converted rice or partially-precooked instant rice for the honest uncooked grain. On the other hand, quality can be found in some convenience foods such as canned or frozen coconut milk found in Asian markets. The concerned oriental cook should never compromise with quality. The finished product can only be as good as the products which go into it.

Jalaja Pradeep's Chicken Tandoori

India

The tandoori-style of cooking originated in Northwestern India in an area of the Punjab which is now Pakistan. Tandoori refers to charcoal cooking, traditionally done in a large jar-shaped clay oven called a tandoor. Searing temperatures inside the oven seals in the juices of meats or chicken instantly; within minutes they cook to juicy perfection. To prepare the chicken for cooking, it is skinned, then marinated in a vermillion-colored spiced-yogurt marinade. Duplicating the cooking conditions in a tandoor isn't possible, but you can still cook authentic tasting Chicken Tandoori on a charcoal grill, a rotisserie or in a heavy roasting pan in a hot oven. Be careful not to overcook the chicken; without the protection of its skin, it can easily dry out. Baste chicken with the marinade to keep it moist. Serve with Grilled Teardrop Bread, page 122.

1 (3- to 3-1/2-lb.) broiler-fryer, cut as instructed, Nonya-Style Grilled Lemon Chicken, page 111
Juice 1 lime or lemon
6 large garlic cloves
1 (3/4-inch-thick) piece fresh gingerroot, sliced
1/3 cup plain yogurt
1/4 teaspoon ground cinnamon
1/2 teaspoon paprika
1/4 teaspoon ground cloves
1/4 teaspoon ground cardamon
1/4 teaspoon red pepper (cayenne)
1/4 teaspoon ground cumin
1/4 teaspoon ground tumeric
1 teaspoon ground coriander
1 teaspoon salt
12 to 14 drops red food coloring, if desired
2 tablespoons Ghee, page 25, or unsalted butter
1 medium-size red Bermuda onion, cut in thin slices

Rinse chicken; remove skin. Pat chicken dry. With a sharp knife, make random slits in chicken. Place chicken in a large shallow baking pan. Squeeze lime juice over chicken; let stand 30 minutes. With motor running of a blender or food processor fitted with the steel blade, drop in garlic and gingerroot. Process until finely minced; add yogurt. Process to a pastelike consistency.

Remove chicken from juice in pan. Combine yogurt mixture, spices, salt and food coloring, if desired, with juice in pan. Rub mixture completely over chicken and into slits. Cover and refrigerate at least 6 hours or overnight. Remove chicken from refrigerator and preheat charcoal grill 30 minutes before cooking.

Sear meaty side of chicken over a hot fire. Reduce fire to moderate heat. Cook, turning several times and basting often with marinade, 25 to 30 minutes or until juices in chicken run clear. Baste with Ghee 5 minutes before chicken is done.

Chicken should be crusty outside, moist and juicy inside. Cut in serving-size pieces. Serve at once with onion. Recipe can be doubled. Makes 4 servings.

HINT
To roast in oven, place chicken on an oiled rack set in a foil-lined roasting pan. Brush with Ghee. Roast in a preheated oven 450F (230C) 10 minutes. Reduce heat to 400F (205C). Roast, basting often with marinade, 20 to 25 minutes more or until juices run clear.

Peking-Style Smoked Turkey with Cornmeal Pancakes

China

The entertaining strategy of mega-active career woman Maggie Mullins is to organize and prepare several failproof courses for a meal in advance. For convenience, prepare Maggie's Peking-style smoked turkey up to three days in advance; refrigerate until one to two hours before serving time.

1 tablespoon salt
1 tablespoon Szechuan peppercorns
1/2 teaspoon five-spice powder
1/4 teaspoon ground cinnamon
1 (10- to 13-lb.) turkey, neck and giblets removed
Sesame seed oil
Thinly sliced peel 2 oranges
Hickory or other wood chips
2 (1/2-inch-thick) slices fresh gingerroot, smashed
3 green onions, smashed
3 whole star anise
1/2 cup water
1/2 cup dry white wine
1 recipe Orange-Flavored Bean Sauce, page 139
Additional green onions, smashed, slivered

Cornmeal Pancakes:
1-3/4 cups all-purpose flour
3/4 cup white cornmeal
1-1/2 cups milk
3/4 cup water
4 large eggs
Vegetable oil

In a small heavy skillet, stir salt and peppercorns over medium heat 2 to 3 minutes or until hot and fragrant. In a small electric coffee mill or blender, grind salt and peppercorns until powdery. Sift mixture into a small bowl. Discard any unground husks. Mix in five-spice powder and cinnamon. Rinse turkey well. Pat dry with paper towels. Rub turkey with sesame seed oil, then with spice mixture. Cover lightly and refrigerate overnight. Remove 1 hour before cooking.

Soak orange peels and hickory chips in water until needed. Preheat a covered grill 30 minutes. Place gingerroot, 3 green onions and star anise inside turkey cavity. Truss turkey. Place a meat thermometer in thickest part of thigh, away from bone. Arrange hot coals on either side of a drip pan placed in center of grate. Pour water and wine into drip pan. Place turkey on an oiled grill rack, breast-side up, directly above drip pan. Add 5 to 6 live coals every hour to maintain cooking temperature.

About 1 hour before end of cooking time, remove drippings from pan; set aside for broth. Place orange peels on hot coals. Add hickory chips at 10 minute intervals. Smoke-cook turkey to 180F (80C) or until a leg moves easily at joint. Remove from grill; let stand 20 to 30 minute before carving in thin slices as needed. Prepare Cornmeal Pancakes; fold in quarters and arrange on a platter. Spread each pancake with Orange-Flavored Bean Sauce. Add turkey and additional green onion. Fold and eat like a taco. Makes 8 to 10 servings.

Cornmeal Pancakes:
In a blender or food processor fitted with the steel blade, blend all ingredients until smooth. Let batter stand 30 minutes. Prepare pancakes; cook as for egg-flour wrappers, Cinnamon-Scented Roast Duck Salad with Egg-Flour Wrappers, pages 64-65, until lightly browned. Makes about 24 pancakes.

Malaysian-Style Satay
Malaysia

Satay (skewered charcoal-grilled meats and seafood) is a popular snack throughout Southeast Asia. There are dozens of variations depending on the geographical location and the cook. My version is adapted from a recipe of Lorna Thiruchandran of Lumut in the state of Perak, Malaysia. For some, the best part of satay is the spicy-hot Satay Peanut Sauce, page 138. Serve satay as a snack, appetizer or main course at a satay party on the patio, allowing guests the fun of grilling their own! If you locate aromatic stalks of fresh lemongrass, crush them at the bulb ends and use them as brushes for basting the skewered meats as they grill.

2 to 2-1/2 pounds beef sirloin (at least 3/4-inch thick), beef flank steak or trimmed
    boned pork loin, partially frozen
1 package bamboo skewers, 8- to 10-inches long, soaked in cold water
1 cup Light Coconut Milk, page 21, or canned coconut milk, slightly diluted
2 tablespoons vegetable oil
1 recipe Satay Peanut Sauce, page 138
1 teaspoon chopped peanuts, if desired
1 teaspoon chopped green onion, if desired
1 recipe Pressed Rice Cakes or Pressed Coconut Rice Cakes, page 73, prepared 1
    to 2 days ahead of serving
2 recipes Hot & Sour Cucumber Sticks, page 133
6 to 8 small red Bermuda onions, cut in wedges

Satay Marinade:
4 stalks fresh lemongrass or 1 tablespoon freshly grated lemon peel
1 teaspoon ground tumeric
1 teaspoon fennel seeds, ground
2 large garlic cloves, finely minced
2 teaspoons finely minced fresh gingerroot
1/3 cup sugar
1/4 cup Indonesian Soy Sauce, page 24, or medium Japanese soy sauce
1 teaspoon salt
2 tablespoons vegetable oil
1/4 teaspoon black pepper
1/4 cup Light Coconut Milk, page 21, or canned coconut milk

Prepare Satay Marinade. With a large sharp knife, slice meat in 1/4-inch-thick slices, then in strips about 2-1/2-inches long and 1-inch wide. With hands, mix meat strips into Satay Marinade in 2 to 3 portions, being sure all meat is coated. Lace seasoned meat strips onto pointed ends of bamboo skewers, leaving 3 to 4 inches at opposite end of skewers for turning on grill. In a large shallow pan, place skewered meat in 1 or 2 layers. Pour on remaining marinade. Refrigerate at least 1 hour or up to 8 hours.

    Preheat charcoal grill 30 minutes. In a small bowl, combine Light Coconut Milk and oil. Grill skewered beef, turning often for even-cooking, 2 to 3 minutes. Baste with coconut milk-oil mixture. Increase cooking time for skewered pork; cook until no longer pink inside. Garnish Satay Peanut Sauce with peanuts and green onion, if desired. Serve satay hot with Satay Peanut Sauce, Pressed Rice Cakes, Hot & Sour Cucumber Sticks and onions. Makes 10 to 12 servings.

Satay Marinade:
If using lemongrass, remove tough outer stalks. Smash inner stalks, thinly slice and mince finely. In a large bowl, combine lemongrass or lemon peel and remaining ingredients. Makes about 3/4 cup.

Chinese-Style Steamed Sandwich Buns   *China*

Evidence of the growth of wheat crops in Northern China dates back to the ancient Yangshao culture, dated around 5000 to 3200 B.C. Bread dough and noodles have been produced in China well over 2,000 years. Wheat is a staple crop of the cold North where rice is difficult to grow. "Man t'ao" (steamed bread) is an important food in the Northern diet. In the South, it is usually served during the "tea-lunch" or as a snack. Basic leavened dough from the Chinese kitchen is not much different from dough prepared in the Western kitchen. Chinese dough doesn't usually contain salt. I added a small amount to improve the taste, to keep a restraint on yeast formation and to strengthen the gluten.

Sesame seed oil
1/3 cup minced green onion, if desired
1/3 cup finely minced country cured or baked ham, if desired
1 tablespoon black Dry Roasted Sesame Seeds, page 24

Basic Chinese Yeast Bread:
1 (1/4-oz.) package active dry yeast (about 1 tablespoon)
1 cup warm water (110F/45C)
1/4 cup sugar
1 teaspoon white vinegar
1 teaspoon salt
2 tablespoons vegetable oil or melted unsalted butter
3 to 3-1/4 cups bleached or unbleached all-purpose flour
Additional vegetable oil

Prepare Basic Chinese Yeast Bread. On a lightly floured surface, roll out 1/2 of dough. With a 4-inch round cutter, cut out dough circles. Spread top of each circle with a small amount of sesame seed oil. Sprinkle with small amounts of green onion and ham, if desired. Fold dough over in half-moon shapes; press lightly to seal. Sprinkle lightly with black Dry Roasted Sesame Seeds. Repeat with remaining dough. Place buns in pans which will fit into a steamer tray, leaving at least 1 inch between buns for expansion. Let stand 15 minutes. In a wok or deep pot, bring 6 cups water to a boil. Place tray over boiling water. Reduce heat to medium-high; steam 10 to 12 minutes or until done. Serve buns warm or at room temperature. Makes 6 to 8 servings.

Basic Chinese Yeast Bread:
Lightly oil a large bowl. In a food processor fitted with the steel blade, process yeast, water and 1 tablespoon of sugar by pressing pulse button on and off several times. Let stand 5 minutes or until foamy. Add remaining sugar, vinegar, salt, 2 tablespoons oil and 2 cups of flour. Process 10 seconds. Add 1 cup of flour; process until a ball of dough forms. If mixture has not formed a ball or is too soft and sticky to continue kneading, sprinkle in 1/4 cup of flour, 1 tablespoon at a time. When ball forms, process 60 seconds.

   Remove steel blade. Oil hands and remove dough. Dough should be soft and velvety. Pat in a smooth rounded shape. Place in oiled bowl. Coat dough very lightly with additional oil to prevent a crust from forming. Cover bowl with a slightly damp kitchen towel. Let rise 1 to 1-1/2 hours or until doubled. Punch down dough; reshape in a smooth rounded ball. Cover again; let rise again about 1 hour or until doubled. On a lightly floured surface, punch down dough. Makes about 1-3/4 pounds dough.

HINT
To prepare dough without a food processor, in a small bowl, mix yeast and water; add sugar. Let stand 5 to 10 minutes or until foamy. Blend in remaining sugar, salt, vinegar and oil. Stir in 2 cups of flour to form a very soft dough. Stir in 1 to 1-1/4 cups more flour until mixture forms a solid ball of dough. On a lightly floured surface, knead dough 10 minutes or until springy and elastic. Add flour as needed to prevent sticking.

Crispy Tissue-Paper Bread   *Southeast Asia*

Crispy thin fried bread rounds are popular in many versions throughout Asia. These are similar to the fried Indian breads called "puris," made with "atta," a fine whole-wheat flour. These ultra-thin, irregular-shaped rounds will blister and sometimes puff up when deep-fried in hot oil. They won't always puff into perfect balloon shapes, but if you have rolled them thin enough, you will love their delicate, crispy texture and spicy taste. A variation, Chinese Mongolian Balloon Bread, is by far the best puffer. Tapping the breads as they fry helps to separate the dough layers, enabling steam to form inside. In turn, this causes puffing. Serve a basketful at your next party for guests to munch on with drinks. The soft touch of Indian spice goes well with many Southeast Asian meals, especially those featuring barbecue. (Photo of *Chinese Mongolian Balloon Bread* on page 119.)

2 cups all-purpose flour, lightly spooned into measuring cup
2 tablespoons whole-wheat flour
1/2 teaspoon salt
1/4 teaspoon black pepper
1/2 teaspoon cumin seeds
1 tablespoon plain yogurt
2 tablespoons vegetable oil
1/2 cup water
Red pepper (cayenne) to taste
6 cups vegetable oil for deep-frying

In a food processor fitted with the steel blade, process flours, salt, black pepper and cumin seeds briefly to mix. In a small bowl, combine yogurt, 2 tablespoons oil and water. With machine running, pour yogurt mixture into flour until it forms a ball. Process dough 1 minute. Remove blade from workbowl. Oil hands lightly; remove dough. On a lightly floured surface, knead dough 10 seconds. Oil dough lightly, cover with a small bowl and let stand 15 minutes.

Shape dough in a 12-inch-long sausage-shaped roll. Cut roll in half. Cut each half in 6 even-size pieces. Dip pieces into flour; press in flattened round discs. Keep covered with a kitchen towel to prevent drying. Roll out 1/2 of discs at a time. Partially roll out 1 disc of dough in an 8-inch tissue-paper-thin round, using flour as needed for rolling. Sprinkle with red pepper. Finish rolling out disc; shape does not have to be perfectly round. Repeat with remaining discs.

In a wok or shallow heavy saucepan, heat 6 cups oil to 385F (195C) or until a 1-inch cube of bread turns golden-brown in 40 seconds. Slip in 1 round at a time. Fry about 30 seconds, tapping gently on dough with back of a wooden spoon. Turn dough; continue frying for a total of 2 to 3 minutes or until bread is light sandy colored, blistered and very crisp. Drain on paper towels. Repeat with remaining rounds. Store in an airtight container. Makes 12 pieces.

VARIATIONS
To prepare *Chinese Mongolian Balloon Bread*, omit black pepper and cumin seeds. Substitue 1 tablespoon of water for yogurt. Substitute wheat germ for whole-wheat flour, if desired.

To prepare *Korean-Style Balloon Bread*, add 1 tablespoon sesame seeds to dry ingredients. Substitute 1 tablespoon sesame seed oil for 1 tablespoon of vegetable oil.

HINT
Texture is best when breads are eaten soon after frying. Recrisp in a preheated oven 250F(120C) about 5 minutes. If desired, heat longer; breads gradually become golden-brown and have a delicious nutty taste after toasting. Watch carefully to prevent burning.

Mongolian Barbecue

North China

When Genghis Kahn and his famous horsemen-warriors swept into China, they introduced the fire-grill method of cooking game and beef. The nomadic warriors lived off the harsh cold lands by stockbreeding and hunting game. The day's hunt would be sliced, marinated and grilled over an open fire. The marinade acted as a preservative, enabling leftovers to be carried safely through the desert. Fire-grilling was highly refined during the Manchurian Dynasty. In the modern-day version, the diner is invited in restaurants throughout Asia to fill a large bowl with an incredible array of raw sliced meats, vegetables, fruits, spices and seasonings. The contents of the bowl is dumped on a giant flat-top indoor fire-grill where it is tossed and cooks in seconds. My presentation is reminiscent of layered Mexican tostados. Sliced, grilled meat and vegetables are heaped onto large paper-thin crispy bread rounds. Choose two or three types of meat to equal the total amount.

1-1/2 pounds beef tenderloin or rib eye, lean boneless pork, lamb or venison,
    partially frozen
1-1/3 cups medium Japanese soy sauce
1-1/3 cups dry white wine
1-1/3 cups beef or chicken stock
1/3 cup sugar
12 green onions, smashed, shredded
1/2 head Nappa cabbage, shredded
2 medium-size carrots, cut in matchstick julienne strips
1 medium-size red bell pepper, cut in matchstick julienne strips
Vegetable oil
1 recipe Chinese Mongolian Balloon Bread, Crispy Tissue-Paper Bread, page 117
1 recipe Basic Cooked White Rice (long- or short-grain), page 22

Condiments:
2 tablespoons grated fresh gingerroot
4 large garlic cloves, finely minced, mixed with 1 tablespoon vegetable oil
Ground Szechuan peppercorns or black pepper
4 green onions, finely minced
Sesame seed oil
Hot chili oil or fresh ground chili paste (sambal oelek)
Red wine vinegar
Fresh cilantro leaves

With a large sharp knife, cut meat in thin slices about 1/8-inch thick. Cut large slices of meat in half; arrange attractively on a large platter. Prepare Condiments. To prepare meat dip, in a large bowl, combine soy sauce, wine, chicken stock and sugar. Arrange onions, cabbage, carrots and bell pepper in separate piles on a serving platter. Provide each guest with a bowl filled with 2/3 cup of meat dip. Season bowls of dip with Condiments to taste.

Heat an electric griddle, electric skillet, wok or heavy skillet over a portable tabletop burner; add a small amount of oil. Invite guests to dip 1 or 2 meat slices into seasoned dip; grill along with a small amount of desired vegetables. Place cooked meat and vegetables on a Chinese Mongolian Balloon Bread. Eat with chopsticks, breaking off pieces of bread. Or fold crispy bread in half and eat like a taco. Serve with Basic Cooked White Rice. Makes 6 servings.

Condiments:
Place Condiments in separate serving bowls.

Mongolian Barbecue; Szechuan Marinated Vegetables, page 132

*To prepare **Korean-Style Grilled Beef Short Ribs**, make a lengthwise cut down the center of the meaty side of the rib to the bone with a sharp knife.*

Make 1 to 2 more cuts through the rib on both sides and lay it open in a strip.

Grilled Sirloin with Thai Hot & Tangy Steak Sauce

Thailand

A real fire-eater's steak sauce! But after the initial heat wave, what fantastic flavor! The hot tangy refreshing flavors of chili peppers, red onion, lime juice, fresh cilantro and fresh mint are blended to enhance the taste of your favorite cut of grilled steak. Tame the fire, if you wish, by eliminating one of the chilies. The sauce amount can be doubled and served as a dressing for a Thai steak salad. To make a Thai steak salad, place thin slices of grilled tender steak on a bed of shredded tender lettuce mixed with fresh basil, fresh mint, cucumber slices and julienne strips of cucumbers and carrots. Spoon steak sauce over the top.

Juice 1 lime or lemon
1 small red Bermuda onion, cut in quarters, sliced paper-thin
2 small fresh whole red chili peppers, stemmed, seeded, minced
3 large garlic cloves, finely minced
1 tablespoon shredded fresh cilantro leaves
1 tablespoon shredded fresh mint leaves
1/4 cup Southeast Asian fish sauce (nampla)
1/4 cup fresh lime juice
1 tablespoon sugar
2-1/2- to 3-pounds boneless beef sirloin
Vegetable oil

To prepare steak sauce, in a medium-size bowl, squeeze juice of 1 lime over onion. Let stand 30 minutes. Pour off and discard lime juice. With a mortar and pestle, grind chili peppers and garlic to a paste or mince as finely as possible. Stir paste, cilantro, mint, fish sauce, 1/4 cup lime juice and sugar into onion; mix well. Cover tightly until needed.

Preheat charcoal grill 30 minutes. Brush beef lightly with oil. Sear on both sides; reduce heat slightly. Continue grilling 10 to 12 minutes or until medium-rare or to desired degree of doneness. Let stand 5 to 10 minutes before carving in thin slices. Spoon steak sauce over each serving. Makes 4 to 5 servings.

Korean-Style Grilled Beef Short Ribs   *Korea*

Beef is the most commonly eaten meat in Korea due to the Mongolian influence from the Central Asian steppes. Koreans prefer their beef marinated in a sweet soy sauce marinade, then quickly grilled over charcoal. Beef short ribs prepared this way are called "bulgalbi"; thinly sliced beef is called "bulgogi." Butterfly the ribs to shorten the cooking time and to allow the marinade to penetrate the meat. The generous amount of sugar is important to the succulent flavor which develops during grilling. Be sure and make plenty; no one ever seems to get enough! Serve with Julienne Pear Salad with Lemon-Sesame Dressing, page 63. And, of course, don't forget plenty of napkins!

> **4 pounds lean beef short ribs, cut 3- to 5-inches long**
> **1 tablespoon sesame seed oil**
>
> *Marinade:*
> **3/4 cup thinly shredded green onion**
> **4 large garlic cloves, finely minced**
> **1 tablespoon finely minced fresh gingerroot**
> **3 tablespoons Dry Roasted Sesame Seeds, page 24**
> **1/2 cup plus 2 tablespoons medium Japanese soy sauce**
> **1/4 cup plus 2 tablespoons sugar**
> **Several dashes black pepper**
> **2 tablespoons brandy, if desired**

Prepare Marinade. With a sharp knife, make a lengthwise cut down center of meaty side of 1 rib to bone. Cut will form 2 pieces of meat still attached to bone. Starting inside cut, make a horizontal cut through 1 piece of meat about 1/2 inch above bone. Do not cut all the way through, detaching meat. Make 1 to 2 more cuts through piece of meat, laying it open in a strip. Repeat on other half of meat in the same way. Lightly score tops of beef strips. Repeat with remaining ribs.

Carefully dip 1 rib at a time into Marinade, coating meat strips. Layer ribs in a large shallow pan. Pour on remaining Marinade. Cover and refrigerate 6 to 8 hours. Remove ribs from refrigerator and preheat charcoal grill 30 minutes before cooking. Mix sesame oil into ribs. Grill ribs, basting occasionally with Marinade, over a hot fire about 20 minutes. Cook until crusty and brown on outside and slightly pink inside or to desired degree of doneness. Or place ribs on a rack set in a foil-lined pan and broil in oven. Makes 4 to 5 servings.

Marinade:
In a medium-size bowl, combine all ingredients. Stir until sugar dissolves.

VARIATION
To prepare *Korean-Style Grilled Spicy Beef*, substitute 1-1/4 to 1-1/2 pounds beef rib eye or other tender beef sliced 1/8-inch thick for short ribs. In a large bowl, prepare 1/2 recipe of Marinade. Dip beef in Marinade; let stand 30 minutes. Grill beef on a preheated hibachi, portable tabletop grill or griddle 1 to 2 minutes or to desired degree of doneness. Makes 4 to 5 servings.

Grilled Teardrop Bread

India

"Naan" is the leavened bread of Northern India. It is served as an accompaniment to meats or chicken prepared the tandoori way, such as Jalaja Pradeep's Chicken Tandoori, page 112. To cook "naan," the baker lowers each round of soft dough into a fiery tandoor oven, then pushes it onto the oven wall for quick cooking. The dough adheres, but sags from its own weight in a teardrop shape. To duplicate the concept of the tandoor oven as closely as possible, broil dough on a preheated hot griddle until the tops are puffy and brown. This combination cooking method helps to quickly cook both sides of the breads at the same time, similar to the tandoor. Although not traditionally done, the slightly hollowed hot breads can be pulled open and stuffed with cheese or grilled meats.

1 (1/4-oz.) package active dry yeast (about 1 tablespoon)
3/4 cup warm water (110F/45C)
2 tablespoons sugar
1/2 cup plus 2 tablespoons Ghee, page 25, or melted butter
1/2 cup plain yogurt, room temperature
1 teaspoon salt
3 cups all-purpose flour
1/2 cup whole-wheat flour
Vegetable oil
Poppy seeds or sesame seeds, if desired

Lightly oil a large bowl. In a medium-size bowl, dissolve yeast in water. Stir in 1 teaspoon of sugar. Let stand 5 to 10 minutes or until foamy. When yeast mixture begins to foam, stir in remaining sugar, 2 tablespoons of Ghee and yogurt. In a food processor fitted with the steel blade, process salt, 2-1/2 cups of all-purpose flour and whole-wheat flour a few seconds to blend. With machine running, pour yeast mixture through feed tube. Process 15 seconds. Add as much of remaining all-purpose flour as needed until mixture forms a ball. If dough causes machine to labor and slow down, sprinkle in all-purpose flour, 1 teaspoon at a time. When a ball forms, process 60 seconds.

Remove steel blade from food processor. Oil hands and remove dough. On a lightly floured surface, knead dough 30 seconds. Smooth in a rounded shape. Rub dough lightly with oil; place in oiled bowl. Cover lightly with a damp kitchen towel. Let dough rise 1 hour or until doubled. Punch down dough; let rise again 1 hour or until doubled.

Place a heavy iron griddle in oven. Preheat oven to 500F (260C). Punch down dough. Roll out dough in a 12-inch-long sausage-shaped roll; cut in half. Cut each half in 6 even-size pieces. Working with 6 pieces of dough, gently pat each dough piece in a ball. Flatten balls; roll out each flattened ball in an elongated teardrop shape about 5-inches long and no more than 1/4-inch thick. Roll top portions about 3-1/4-inches wide. Taper bottom portions in a rounded point. Brush both sides of dough with 1/2 cup of Ghee. Sprinkle with poppy seeds, if desired.

Lay as many pieces of dough as will fit on extremely hot griddle. Broil dough 4 to 5 minutes or until slightly puffed and dark golden-brown. Turn over and brown other side. Repeat with remaining pieces of dough. Serve warm. Makes 12 small breads.

*To prepare **Grilled Teardrop Bread**, form the dough in elongated teardrop shapes and place on a hot griddle. Broil until the tops are puffy and golden-brown.*

Indonesian-Style Butterfly Leg of Lamb with Satay Peanut Sauce   *Indonesia*

What could be more succulent than grilled fresh young leg of lamb, conveniently butterflied by your butcher for quick cooking and easy carving. The fragrant marinade adds extra flavor and helps keep it moist.

> 2 stalks fresh lemongrass or freshly grated peel 1 lemon
> 1/4 cup Indonesian Soy Sauce, page 24
> 2 tablespoons fresh lime or lemon juice
> 3 tablespoons vegetable oil
> 1 teaspoon ground cumin
> 1 teaspoon salt
> 2 large garlic cloves, finely minced
> 1/4 teapoon red pepper (cayenne)
> 1 (5- to 6-lb.) leg of lamb, fat trimmed, boned, butterflied
> 1 recipe Satay Peanut Sauce, page 138

To make marinade, if using lemongrass, remove tough outer stalks. Smash inner stalks, thinly slice and mince finely. In a large nonaluminum roasting pan, combine lemongrass or lemon peel, Indonesian Soy Sauce, lime juice, oil, cumin, salt, garlic and red pepper.

Coat lamb completely in marinade. Cover and refrigerate at least 8 hours or up to 24 hours. Remove lamb from refrigerator and preheat grill 30 minutes before cooking. Brush grill with vegetable oil. Grill lamb, turning occasionally and basting with marinade, over a hot fire 30 to 35 minutes or until crusty outside and slightly pink inside or to desired degree of doneness. Let stand 10 minutes before carving in thin slices. Warm Satay Peanut Sauce. Serve lamb with peanut sauce. Makes 6 to 8 servings.

Dee's Spicy Grilled Lamb Pockets *Pakistan*

Having lived six years in Southeast Asia, my sister Dee Bradney and her husband Paul like to entertain oriental-style. Guests love to be invited to one of their famous Southeast Asian patio buffets featuring a smorgasbord of grilled meats and seafood. Everyone raves about the spicy grilled lamb pockets. They are great for easy entertaining; shape the meat patties hours ahead for last minute grilling. Serve with your favorite side dishes, including perhaps Farida's Fried Eggplant in Spiced Yogurt Sauce, page 59, and a platter filled with refreshing sliced fresh fruits.

8 (4-inch) mini-pita bread rounds
Red leaf lettuce
1 recipe Jade-Mint Raita, page 130, or sour cream

Cucumber-Onion Relish:
1 European-style cucumber, peeled, cut in half lengthwise
1 medium-size red Bermuda onion, cut in half, thinly sliced
1/4 cup fresh cilantro or mint leaves, shredded
1 small fresh whole green chili pepper, stemmed, seeded, minced
1/4 teaspoon salt
Juice 1 large lemon or lime

Spicy Ground Lamb Kebabs:
2 pounds ground lamb or ground beef
2 tablespoons water
1 medium-size onion, finely minced
2 garlic cloves, finely minced
1/4 cup finely minced fresh parsley
2 tablespoons shredded fresh cilantro leaves
1 large egg
1 teaspoon salt
1/4 teaspoon black pepper
1/2 teaspoon ground cinnamon
1/8 teaspoon ground coriander
1 teaspoon ground cumin
1/2 teaspoon red pepper (cayenne) or to taste

Preheat charcoal grill 30 minutes. Prepare Cucumber-Onion Relish and Spicy Ground Lamb Kebabs. Divide Spicy Ground Lamb Kebabs in 8 portions; shape in 8 flat round patties. Slice open tops of pita bread rounds; wrap in foil. Place on grill to warm. Grill meat patties over a hot fire 4 to 5 minutes on each side or to desired degree of doneness. Fold a lettuce leaf around each pattie; stuff into warmed pita-bread rounds. Spoon Cucumber-Onion Relish and Jade-Mint Raita into pockets. Serve at once. Makes 8 stuffed lamb pockets.

Cucumber-Onion Relish:
Scrape seeds out of cucumber halves and discard. Cut crosswise in paper-thin slices. In a medium-size bowl, combine cucumber and remaining ingredients; mix well. Let stand 30 minutes. Drain well. Or cover and refrigerate several hours until needed; drain before serving. Makes 8 servings.

Spicy Ground Lamb Kebabs:
In a medium-size bowl, combine all ingredients. Makes about 2 pounds.

SAUCES, DIPS & CONDIMENTS

Tangy dipping sauces, crunchy pickled vegetables and fruit-filled chutneys are only a few types of accompaniments or little side dishes which play a supporting role in Asian meals. They serve to add colorful visual excitement, stimulate the palate and provide a contrasting yet complimentary range of taste sensations. A few of the accompaniments in this chapter have been paired with primary dishes in partnerships of long-standing traditions. Satay Peanut Sauce, page 138, is a suberb dipping sauce for grilled Malaysian-Style Satay, page 114. Crispy Fried Onions with Coconut & Peanuts, page 126, is a splendid relish which is used to add flavor, crunch and color to plain white cooked rice in a Southeast Asian meal.

All of the accompaniments are versatile and can accompany a wide range of primary dishes. Curried Pear Chutney with Fresh Ginger, page 128, is usually paired off with Indian curried dishes, but is equally delicious with smoked turkey, baked ham or roast pork. The ever-changing range of flavors in this outstanding chutney will linger in your memory long after the last spoonful is gone.

In Asia, vegetables have been pickled in briny vinegar since ancient times. In China and Japan, they were once pickled solely as a means of food preservation, especially important during cold barren winters. It was discovered that preserving methods greatly intensified the flavors of vegetables. They were tempting enough to be eaten as a primary food themselves, offering a lively flavor and textural contrast to a bowl of plain white rice.

Sometimes pickled vegetables were added to cooked dishes, giving them a flavor boost as well. Pickled vegetables also provided important nutritional value during cold winter months. Lemon-Cucumber Sunomono, page 131, is a traditional Japanese vinegared side dish which will add a pleasant lemony-crunch to any meal. Szechuan Marinated Vegetables, page 132, offers a bold spicy-hot taste as well as crunch. They are addictive; once you start nibbling on them you will find it hard to stop. Colorful Vietnamese Pickled Julienne of Vegetables, page 134, adds a sweet-tart flavor and crunchiness to the intense-flavored Nuoc Cham Dipping Sauce, page 136, which is Viet Nam's standard table dip. Plum Brandy Sauce, page 136, is an excellent dipping sauce for crisp-fried Asian pastries or can be used as a basting sauce for roast poultry or baked ham.

Crispy Fried Onions
with Coconut & Peanuts

Indonesia

You will be tempted to eat this crispy sambal or relish as a snack! It is served throughout Indonesia and Malaysia as a topping to be sprinkled on top of rice and noodle dishes and meat or poultry dishes cooked in coconut milk. Make the relish ahead and store in an airtight container.

1 large white onion, cut in half, sliced paper-thin
1 large red Bermuda onion, cut in half, sliced paper-thin
1 teaspoon salt
1/4 cup vegetable oil
2 large garlic cloves, minced
1 cup shredded unsweetened coconut
1/2 cup dry roasted peanuts, coarsely chopped
1/3 cup golden raisins
1/2 teaspoon freshly grated lemon peel
2 tablespoons brown sugar
1/2 teaspoon ground cumin
1 tablespoon fresh lime or lemon juice
1/4 red pepper (cayenne) or to taste

Spread onions on several layers of paper towels. Sprinkle with salt. Let stand 10 minutes or until moisture is released. Gently press out moisture. Pat onions dry with paper towels. In a large skillet, heat oil over low heat until hot. Add onions and garlic. Fry slowly, stirring often, about 30 minutes or until golden-brown and reduced in size. Stir in coconut, peanuts and raisins. Increase heat slightly. Cook, stirring often, 10 to 15 minutes or until coconut is lightly browned and onions are dry and crispy. Stir in lemon peel, brown sugar, cumin, lime juice and red pepper. Cook 5 minutes or until dry. Cool and store in an airtight container. Makes about 2 cups.

VARIATION
Substitute shredded sweetened coconut for shredded unsweetened coconut. Omit brown sugar.

Oven-Baked Cranberry-Cardamon Chutney

You will appreciate this easy method, which seems so well suited to my busy life, for preparing oven-baked chutney. Start the chutney on top of the range and once in the oven, forget it until it's done. If you are a cranberry-lover, you will enjoy the tanginess they lend to this cardamon-scented relish. Serve with curried dishes, roasted poultry or pork. Blend the chilled chutney with equal parts of Creme Fraîche, page 22, plain yogurt or whipped cream for a wonderful topping for Meiko's Ginger-Flavored Sweet Wine Cake, page 147, or sliced fresh fruit. Store several packs of seasonal fresh cranberries in the freezer to be able to make Oven-Baked Cranberry-Cardamon Chutney year-round.

1 large navel orange, unpeeled, cut in small pieces
1 cup top-quality red currant, raspberry or plum jelly
1 cup packed light-brown sugar
Freshly grated peel 1 medium-size lime or lemon
2 tablespoons fresh lime or lemon juice
12 ounces fresh whole cranberries
2 tart green apples, peeled, cored, diced
2 (1/8-inch-thick) slices fresh gingerroot, finely minced
2/3 cup golden raisins
1 (2-inch) cinnamon stick
1/4 teaspoon freshly grated nutmeg
1/4 teaspoon ground allspice
Pinch salt
2 teaspoons green cardamon pods or 1/2 teaspoon ground cardamon
3 tablespoons toasted chopped almonds
2 tablespoons orange liqueur, if desired

In a blender or food processor fitted with the steel blade, process orange until finely ground. In a large ovenproof saucepan, combine orange and juice, jelly and brown sugar. Cook over low heat until jelly is melted. Stir in lime peel and juice, cranberries, apples, gingerroot, raisins, spices and salt.

Preheat oven to 350F (175C). In a mortar, pound cardamon seeds with a pestle to break open pods and release seeds. Continue pounding and grinding until seeds are pulverized; sift through a fine sieve into a small bowl. Discard pods; measure 1/2 teaspoon ground seeds. Blend into fruit mixture.

Tightly cover and bake in preheated oven 1-1/2 hours. Stir in almonds. Remove cinnamon stick. Cool to room temperature. Stir in orange liqueur, if desired. Refrigerate and chill in an airtight container to mellow and enhance flavors. Store in refrigerator up to several weeks. Makes about 3-1/4 cups.

Curried Pear Chutney with Fresh Ginger   *India*

Food historians tell us pear seeds were found in early Chinese tombs around 2000 years B. C. A member of the rose family, pears provide wonderful textural background for the rich flavors in this piquant relish, especially if you choose slightly underripe ones with a firm resilence. Anjou, Comice and Bartlett are good choices. Julienne strips of fresh gingerroot add a burst of flavor. The spices cardamon, tumeric and cumin combine to create the taste of a delicate "masala," an Indian spice blend. A touch of pear liqueur or dark rum adds a mellow, warm bouquet. Each bite is everchanging. Serve this rich dark-amber chutney with curries and poultry dishes, especially roast duck. Surprise the mincemeat lovers in your family and substitute this curried pear chutney the next time you bake mincemeat cake or cookies.

1 cup white cider vinegar
2-1/2 cups packed light-brown sugar
1/2 cup orange honey
3 tablespoons fine julienne strips fresh gingerroot
Juice and fine julienne strips of peel 1 medium-size lime
1 (2-inch) cinnamon stick
1/4 teaspoon ground tumeric
1/2 teaspoon ground cloves
1/2 teaspoon red pepper (cayenne)
1/8 teaspoon ground nutmeg
1/4 teaspoon ground cumin
3 whole cardamon seeds, slightly crushed
1/4 teaspoon salt
3 tablespoons finely diced red bell pepper
4 pounds firm unblemished green pears, peeled, cut in quarters, cored, cut in
  1/2-inch cubes
1 cup golden raisins or 1/2 cup golden raisins and 1/2 cup dark raisins
2 teaspoons tamarind concentrate mixed with 2 tablespoons water or lime juice
  to taste
2 tablespoons pear liqueur or dark rum, if desired

In a large saucepan, combine vinegar, brown sugar, orange honey, gingerroot, lime juice and peel, cinnamon stick, spices, salt and bell pepper. Bring to a boil over medium-high heat, stirring constantly to dissolve honey and sugar. Add pears; bring back to a boil, stirring well to coat pears.

   Turn off heat. Let mixture stand 1 hour. Bring to a boil; reduce heat to medium-low. Simmer, uncovered, 30 minutes. Add raisins. Continue simmering 1 hour or until chutney is deep-golden and greatly reduced to a thick conserve. Stir in tamarind water and pear liqueur, if desired. Makes 1 quart.

Fresh pears and gingerroot combine with spices and rum to make **Curried Pear Chutney with Fresh Ginger.**

Serve this rich dark-amber chutney over roast duck for an exciting taste surprise.

Five-Spice Nuts
China

These crunchy fragrant nuts are great for appetizers or snacks. Use in place of plain peanuts in stir-fried dishes, fried rice dishes or baking. Friends always love to recieve a jarful as a gift with a recipe card filled with ideas for using them tied on the side. If you ever have a cup left over, process in a food processor a few minutes and presto—five-spice peanut butter!

> **1/2 teaspoon five-spice powder**
> **1/2 teaspoon ground cinnamon**
> **2 tablespoons sugar**
> **1 (8-oz.) jar dry roasted peanuts**
> **1 to 2 tablespoons sesame seed oil or as needed**

Preheat oven to 325F (165C). In a small bowl, combine five-spice powder, cinnamon, sugar and peanuts. Drizzle with enough sesame seed oil to moisten nuts sufficiently so spices will adhere. On a baking sheet, spread coated nuts and any moistened loose spices. Bake, stirring 1 to 2 times, 15 minutes or until nuts are hot and spices become aromatic. Cool nuts; repack into original airtight container. To freshen taste, reheat nuts in a preheated 325F (165C) oven until warm. Makes 1 (8-oz.) jar.

Jade-Mint Raita

India

This creamy yogurt-based sauce is especially refreshing with the special flavor of fresh mint. Use it as a dressing spooned over sliced fresh tomato and cucumber. For a filling, low-calorie salad, blend raita into half a pound of cooked pasta such as rice-shaped pasta or small rings. Be sure to try it in the more traditional Indian style such as the variation noted below. In that method, diced pieces of red onion, tomato and cucumber are folded into the mint-flavored raita. Prepared either way, mint raita is an excellent accompaniment to hot and spicy curry dishes or grilled meats and poultry.

    1/3 cup stemmed tightly packed fresh mint leaves
    2 cups plain yogurt
    1/4 generous cup Crème Fraîche, page 22, or sour cream
    1/2 teaspoon salt or to taste
    1/2 teaspoon sugar
    1/4 teaspoon white pepper
    2 tablespoons chopped red onion
    Fresh mint leaves

In a blender or food processor fitted with the steel blade, process 1/3 cup mint leaves until finely chopped. Add yogurt; process to a puree. In a medium-size bowl, combine puree, Crème Fraîche, salt, sugar and white pepper. Cover and refrigerate at least 1 hour or overnight. Garnish with onion and mint leaves. Makes about 2-1/2 cups.

VARIATIONS
Increase onion to 1 small red onion, chopped. In a medium-size bowl, combine onion, 1 medium-size tomato, seeded and chopped, and 1/2 European-style cucumber, peeled and chopped, with mint raita.

To use as a dressing for fresh fruit, omit onion.

Lemon-Ginger Dressing

Lemon-ginger flavored mayonnaise can be used in dozens of recipes, including those for making "sushi" or seafood and pasta salads. To make foolproof mayonnaise, be sure the eggs are at room temperature and that initially the oil is added in droplets to the beaten egg. This will allow the mixture to emulsify properly and enable the eggs to hold the oil in a thick suspension.

    1 large egg, room temperature
    1 tablespoon rice vinegar
    1/4 teaspoon salt or to taste
    1 generous teaspoon freshly grated lemon peel
    2 to 3 teaspoons fresh ginger juice
    1 cup almond or top-quality vegetable oil

In a blender or food processor fitted with the steel blade, process egg 15 seconds. Add vinegar, salt, lemon peel and ginger juice; process 5 seconds. With machine running, drizzle 1/2 of oil in egg mixture. Add remaining oil in a slow steady stream. Dressing will become thick. Refrigerate in an airtight container or a squeeze-tube bottle, which is handy when making sushi, up to 5 days. Makes about 1-1/8 cups.

Lemon-Cucumber Sunomono   *Japan*

Small, thin-skinned Japanese cucumbers have fewer seeds and a garden-fresh taste. If you can't find them, substitute one European-style cucumber for two or three Japanese cucumbers. Prepared "sunomono-style," thinly sliced cucumbers are softened through moderate salting, then rinsed and seasoned in a flavored vinegar dressing. In the rinsing step, a portion of the dressing is used to wash away salty juices and add flavor. Generally classified as salads, "Sunomono" dishes are always served in minute portions. I often serve them as pickles, to add crunch and a refreshing taste to any Asian meal. Sometimes I dress the cucumbers up in a more salad-like fashion, mixing in small amounts of lump crabmeat or cooked, sliced shrimp. Thin strips of smoked salmon or blanched squid also make delicious additions.

2 European-style cucumbers
1 to 2 tablespoons salt
2 teaspoons white hulled Dry Roasted Sesame Seeds, page 24

Tangy Dressing:
1/2 cup rice vinegar
1/2 cup Japanese soup stock (dashi) or water
1/4 cup fresh lemon juice
3 tablespoons sugar
1 tablespoon medium Japanese soy sauce
1 teaspoon grated fresh gingerroot
Freshly grated peel 1/2 lemon

To brighten skin, pour ample boiling water over whole cucumbers in a strainer. Immediately drop into iced water. When well-chilled, remove cucumbers and pat dry with paper towels. Trim cucumber ends; cut in half lengthwise. With a spoon, scrape out and discard seeds. Cut cucumber halves crosswise in paper-thin slices. Place slices in a strainer set over a bowl; mix in salt. Let cucumbers stand 10 minutes to soften and slightly wilt fibers.

Prepare Tangy Dressing. Gently press cucumber slices in strainer to drain liquids. Rinse cucumbers to remove excess salt by pouring 1/3 to 1/2 of dressing over them in strainer. Press cucumbers again; remove to a medium-size bowl. Carefully combine with remaining dressing. With fingers, lift small amounts of cucumber out of dressing. Shake off dressing; place small mounds on tiny serving plates. Sprinkle each serving with white Dry Roasted Sesame Seeds. Serve at once. Makes 8 to 10 small servings.

Tangy Dressing:
In a small bowl, combine all ingredients. Makes about 1-1/2 cups.

HINT
After rinsing step, cucumbers can be refrigerated 2 to 3 hours in a covered container. Chill dressing. Combine cucumbers and dressing just before serving.

Szechuan Marinated Vegetables   *China*

Colorful miniature vegetables and sliced vegetables are pickled in a zesty marinade. As you serve the tasty vegetables, replenish the storage jar of Szechuan Marinade with fresh unpickled vegetables. (Photo on pages 75 and 119.)

    1 bunch miniature carrots, scraped, ends trimmed
    1 medium-size green bell pepper, ends trimmed, seeded, ribs removed, cut in
        3/4-inch strips
    1 medium-size red bell pepper, ends trimmed, seeded, ribs removed, cut in
        3/4-inch strips
    1 medium-size yellow bell pepper, ends trimmed, seeded, ribs removed, cut in
        3/4-inch strips
    1 (1-lb.) can miniature corn, rinsed in cool water, drained
    3 to 4 small fresh whole red chili peppers, stemmed, slit open on 1 side
    3 large garlic cloves, smashed, cut in half
    2 (1/8-inch-thick) slices fresh gingerroot, smashed, cut in half

    Szechuan Marinade:
    1-1/2 cups water
    1-1/2 cups rice vinegar
    1-1/2 cups sugar
    1 teaspoon salt

Prepare Szechuan Marinade. In a large glass jar with a tight-fitting lid, arrange vegetables attractively, distributing chili peppers, garlic and gingerroot evenly throughout. Pour Szechuan Marinade over vegetables; attach lid. Refrigerate overnight. Remove vegetables from marinade with a slotted spoon. Arrange on a serving dish. Vegetables will keep well up to 1 week. Makes 6 to 8 servings.

Szechuan Marinade:
In a medium-size bowl, combine all ingredients. Stir until sugar dissolves. Makes about 1 quart.

    VARIATION
    Substitute 3 large carrots, cut in 2-inch strips for miniature carrots.

Have you ever wondered why the fiery taste of chili peppers is addictive to so many people? Chili peppers contain capsaicin, an alkaloid which acts as an irritant and causes the burning sensation when you bite into chili-laden foods. It also acts as a digestive stimulant and promotes prespiration. It is believed that sweating caused by high consumption of hot chilies helps to cool down the body, especially important in hot tropical climates. One theory on the popularity of chili peppers states that the taste of capsaicin in hot chilies jolts the body into pleasurable shock, possibly releasing endorphins, or opiate substances from the brain.

Hot & Sour Cucumber Sticks   *China*

Cucumbers marinated in vinegar are eaten in a variety of ways throughout the world. They are a favorite summertime salad at home in Tennessee, sometimes scented with fresh garden herbs or prepared in a sassy version with sweet onion rings and plenty of Tennessee hot sauce. Throughout Asia, I discovered dozens of variations of marinated cucumbers. Whatever the seasonings, sugar or honey were usually added to enhance the vinegar flavor and soften the acidity. Besides cucumbers and vinegar, I vary the supporting ingredients according to the origin of accompanying dishes and the season. A few favorite additions include minced garlic, gingerroot, mint, cilantro and fresh fruits such as pineapple, kiwifruit or crunchy, tart pomegranate seeds. These cool little salads will provide interesting textural contrast to meals. (Photo on pages 115 and 135.)

2 European-style cucumbers, ends trimmed, cut in half lengthwise
1/2 teaspoon sesame seed oil
2 teaspoons black Dry Roasted Sesame Seeds, page 24
Pomegranate seeds, if desired

Hot & Sour Dressing:
1 cup rice vinegar
1/2 cup sugar
3/4 teaspoon salt
2 small fresh whole red chili peppers, stemmed, cut in half lengthwise, seeded,
   ribs removed

With a small spoon, scrape out and discard seeds in each cucumber half. Cut each half lengthwise down middle in 2 to 3 long strips. Cut strips in 1-1/2-inch-long sticks. Prepare Hot & Sour Dressing. Stir in cucumber sticks. Cover and refrigerate at least 1 hour or up to 6 hours. Stir in sesame seed oil up to 30 minutes before serving . With a slotted spoon, remove cucumbers sticks and chili peppers to a serving dish. Remove peppers, if desired. Sprinkle with black Dry Roasted Sesame Seeds and pomegranate seeds, if desired. Serve at once. Makes 6 servings.

Hot & Sour Dressing:
In a large bowl, combine all ingredients. Stir well until sugar is dissolved. Makes about 1-1/4 cups.

VARIATIONS
To prepare *Thai-Style Hot & Sour Cucumbers*, cut 4 seeded cucumber halves crosswise in 1/4-inch-thick slices. Stir 1 small red onion, cut in half and thinly sliced, 2 tablespoons chopped fresh mint and 2 tablespoons chopped fresh cilantro into cucumbers and dressing.

To prepare *Indonesian-Style Hot & Sour Cucumbers*, cut 4 seeded cucumber halves lengthwise down middle in 8 strips. Cut strips crosswise in 1/2-inch pieces. Stir 3/4 cup chopped pineapple cubes, 1 tablespoon fresh lime juice, 1/2 teaspoon freshly grated lime peel, 1/2 teaspoon grated fresh gingerroot and 1 tablespoon chopped dried shrimp, if desired, into cucumbers and dressing.

Vietnamese Pickled Julienne of Vegetables

Viet Nam

These crisp, tangy pickled vegetables are an essential addition to the everyday Vietnamese dipping sauce, "nuoc cham." They are so refreshing you might keep a jarful on hand to scatter over your favorite green and pasta salads or just to enjoy as a tasty snack.

> **2 cups rice vinegar**
> **1 cup water**
> **1-1/2 cups sugar**
> **2 to 3 medium-size carrots, diagonally cut in paper-thin slices, cut in 1-1/2-inch matchstick julienne strips**
> **1 (3-inch) piece Japanese white radish (daikon), peeled, cut in paper-thin slices, cut in 1-1/2-inch matchstick julienne strips**
> **1/2 small green bell pepper, if desired, ends trimmed, seeded, ribs removed, cut in 1-1/2-inch matchstick julienne strips**
> **1/2 small yellow bell pepper, if desired, ends trimmed, seeded, ribs removed, cut in 1-1/2-inch matchstick julienne strips**

In a medium-size saucepan, combine vinegar, water and sugar. Cook over medium heat until hot and sugar is dissolved. Remove from heat; cool completely. Pour mixture into a large glass jar with a tight-fitting lid. Add julienne-cut vegetables. Attach lid and refrigerate overnight. As vegetables are removed from marinade for use, more vegetables can be added, if desired. Makes 1 quart.

Sweet & Spicy Dip for Fresh Fruit

Thailand

A most unusual dip and remarkably delicious! I dared not title this recipe Fish-Sauce Dip for fear most people would continue flipping right past this page! But fish sauce is the primary flavor, although you might not realize it from your first taste. The fish sauce is diluted with caramel syrup which softens its distinctive flavor. On the other hand, the salty fish sauce cuts the sweetness of the syrup. The unlikely addition of minced onion adds a nice taste and textural contrast, resulting in an elusive but pleasant taste. A strange marriage but an altogether happy union! Serve with slices of chilled mango, crisp green apples, pears or apple-pears for dipping. This is also delicious with Deep Fried Shrimp Chips, page 71, or won ton or gyoza wrappers which have been fried to crispy chips.

> **2 recipes Thin Caramel Syrup, page 27**
> **1/4 cup Southeast Asian fish sauce (nampla)**
> **1 tablespoon finely minced shallot or red Bermuda onion**
> **2 teaspoons fresh lime juice**
> **1/8 teaspoon red pepper (cayenne) or to taste**

In a medium-size bowl, combine all ingredients. Serve at once or use within 3 hours. Cover and refrigerate leftover dip. Makes about 1-1/4 cups.

VARIATION
Mix 1 tablespoon finely chopped peanuts into sauce. Use as a dressing for green salads.

From top: Vietnamese Pickled Julienne of Vegetables; Hot & Sour Cucumber Sticks, page 133; Sweet & Spicy Dip for Fresh Fruit

Plum Brandy Sauce

This fruity sauce is an excellent dipping sauce for Southeast Asian pastries or for basting poultry or pork grilled over charcoal.

> **2 tablespoons prepared chili sauce**
> **1 cup plum jam or preserves**
> **1 cup apricot jam or preserves**
> **1/8 teaspoon five-spice powder**
> **1/4 teaspoon salt**
> **3 tablespoons vinegar or to taste**
> **1/4 cup packed brown sugar**
> **1 tablespoon thin Japanese soy sauce or 1-1/2 teaspoons medium Japanese**
> **   soy sauce**
> **Freshly grated peel and juice 1 orange**
> **2 teaspoons cornstarch**
> **3 tablespoons brandy**

In a medium-size saucepan, combine chili sauce, jams, five-spice powder, salt, vinegar, brown sugar, soy sauce and orange peel. Cook, stirring often, over medium-low heat until jams are melted. In a small bowl, combine orange juice and cornstarch; stir into sauce mixture. Continue cooking, stirring constantly, 1 minute or until slightly thickened. Pour into a serving bowl; cool slightly. Stir in brandy. Makes about 2-1/2 cups.

Nuoc Cham Dipping Sauce   *Viet Nam*

"Nuoc mam" is a salty thin fish sauce used extensively as a seasoning in the Vietnamese cuisine, much the way soy sauce is used in Chinese and Japanese cuisines. Like top-quality fish sauces of other Southeast Asian cuisines, it has a distinctive yet pleasant taste which ever-so-subtly enhances the flavors of foods. Unfortunately, "nuoc mam" is not presently available in the United States. However, fish sauce from other countries can be sucessfully substituted, preferably "nampla" from Thailand or "patis" from the Philippines. Use fish sauce to make "nuoc cham," the everyday dipping sauce on Vietnamese tables. My Vietnamese friend and restaurant owner, Ai Ba Li, says, "Good fish sauce is an extraordinary seasoning for foods; it is so delicious it would make Chanel Number 5 taste good!"

> **1/2 cup Southeast Asian fish sauce (nampla)**
> **1/2 cup water**
> **1 to 2 tablespoons fresh lime juice**
> **2 tablespoons sugar**
> **2 garlic cloves, finely minced**
> **1 to 2 small fresh whole red chili peppers, stemmed, seeded, minced**
> **1 to 2 tablespoons Vietnamese Pickled Julienne of Vegetables, page 134**

In a medium-size bowl, combine all ingredients except Vietnamese Pickled Julienne of Vegetables. Let stand 30 minutes or longer for flavors to blend. Strain sauce into a small bowl, if desired. Stir in pickled vegetables. Tightly cover and refrigerate leftover sauce. Makes 1 cup.

Cranberry-Orange Dipping Sauce

Serve this tangy fruit sauce with fried filled Asian pastries or meatballs. It's a wonderful dipping sauce for Shanghaied Chicken Nuggets, page 32.

2 cups sugar
1 cup water
1 pound fresh whole cranberries
1/2 cup orange or apricot preserves
3 to 4 tablespoons fresh lemon juice
1/3 cup fresh orange juice
1/2 teaspoon ground cloves
1/4 teaspoon five-spice powder
1/2 teaspoon ground cinnamon

In a medium-size saucepan, combine sugar, water and cranberries over medium heat; simmer until cranberry skins pop open. Press mixture through a fine strainer into a medium-size bowl; discard skins. Return cranberry puree to saucepan. Add orange preserves, lemon and orange juice, cloves, five-spice powder and cinnamon. Cook over low heat until preserves melt. Serve warm. Or cover and refrigerate until needed. Reheat over low heat before serving. Makes about 4 cups.

Chinese Red Hot Sauce   *Singapore*

This bright-red sauce gets its firepower from Indonesian ground fresh chili paste, available at most Asian markets. I like to use a popular brand made in Los Angeles. Look for the colorful red mixture in the clear plastic jars labeled "sambal oelek." Made with fresh red chilies, water, vinegar and salt, the paste is extremely fiery, but adds delicious flavor to foods. Use about one-half teaspoon in place of one tiny chili pepper. Serve with fried snacks or seafood. It will add a peppery glow to many other favorite foods; try adding some to your next meatloaf mixture.

1/2 cup ketchup
1/2 cup prepared chili sauce
1 teaspoon soy sauce
1 garlic clove, finely minced
1 teaspoon finely minced fresh gingerroot
1 tablespoon ground fresh chili paste (sambal oelek)
1 tablespoon sugar
1 tablespoon fresh lemon juice

In a medium-size bowl, combine all ingredients. Use at once or cover and refrigerate until needed. Makes about 1 cup.

Satay Peanut Sauce

Malaysia

Chili-hot peanut sauce is the most popular sauce served with Southeast Asian satay (skewered grilled meats and seafood). This recipe produces a sauce base which can be thinned with coconut milk to the desired consistency. For convenience, make it with top-quality peanut butter as some good cooks do in Malaysia today. The original recipe for this sauce called for twenty to twenty-five dried chilies; adjust the suggested amounts to suit your own fire-eating abilities. (Photo on page 115.)

> **2 stalks fresh lemongrass or freshly grated peel 1 large lemon**
> **1/4 cup peanut or vegetable oil**
> **2 to 3 small fresh whole red chili peppers, stemmed, seeded, minced**
> **5 shallots, finely minced**
> **1 large garlic clove, finely minced**
> **1/4 cup whole macadamia nuts or whole blanched almonds, finely ground almost to a paste consistency**
> **1/2 teaspoon ground cumin**
> **1-1/2 teaspoons ground coriander**
> **1/2 teaspoon ground fennel**
> **1/2 cup roasted peanuts, ground to peanut butter or 1/3 cup top-quality peanut butter**
> **3 cups Light Coconut Milk, page 21, or canned coconut milk**
> **1 tablespoon Indonesian Soy Sauce, page 24, or medium Japanese soy sauce**
> **1 tablespoon brown sugar**
> **2 teaspoons tamarind concentrate or juice 1/2 lime or lemon**
> **1/2 cup water**
> **1/2 teaspoon roasted dried fish paste (blachan) or 1 teaspoon Southeast Asian fish sauce (nampla), if desired.**
> **Salt to taste**

If using lemongrass, remove tough outer stalks. Smash inner stalks, thinly slice and mince finely. In a wok or medium-size saucepan, heat oil over medium heat until hot. Add lemongrass or lemon peel, chili peppers, shallots and garlic; fry 3 to 4 minutes or until shallots are light golden-brown. Add ground nut paste, cumin, coriander and fennel. Cook, stirring constantly, 1 minute. Reduce heat slightly. Stir in peanut butter until melted. Stir in 1-1/2 cups of Light Coconut Milk, Indonesian Soy Sauce and brown sugar.

In a small bowl, dissolve tamarind concentrate in water; stir into sauce. Add fish paste, if desired, and salt. Increase heat slightly. Simmer 10 minutes or until oils come to top of sauce. Stir often; scrape down sides of pan. To serve immediately, stir in remaining coconut milk to desired sauce consistency. Or cool sauce base, cover tightly and refrigerate up to 4 days. Reheat as needed, thinning with coconut milk. Serve warm. Makes 3 to 3-1/2 cups.

HINT
Sauce can be processed in a blender or food processor fitted with the steel blade for a smoother textured sauce.

*To prepare **Satay Peanut Sauce**, remove the tough outer stalks of the lemongrass and smash the tender inner stalks.*

Orange-Flavored Bean Sauce   *Korea*

"Kochu jang" (Korean-style bean paste) is the distant cousin of an early Chinese prototype which existed long before the Chou Dynasty (722-481 B.C.). The original flavor was created from a combination of seafood, animal parts and salt. The rather distinctive-tasting, fermented mash gradually evolved into the mild, delicious soybean-based products we know and love today. Soy sauce originated as a by-product of some of the early forms of soybean mash. Other modern day cousins are Japanese miso paste and Chinese hoisin sauce. Use them interchangeably with the Korean bean paste called for in this recipe. Made with red peppers and sweet rice, "kochu jang" leaves a lingering sweetness and rich flavor in your mouth, as well as the bite of real heat!

> **1/2 cup Korean-style bean paste (kochu jang)**
> **1 tablespoon red wine vinegar**
> **2 tablespoons fresh orange juice**
> **2 tablespoons sugar**
> **Freshly grated peel 1 small orange**

In a small bowl, combine all ingredients until smooth. Serve at once or cover and refrigerate until needed. Makes 3/4 cup.

Garlic & Vinegar Dipping Sauce

Southeast Asia

This tangy, garlic-flavored dipping sauce can be used for a variety of crispy fried snacks. Try it with Shrimp & Pork Rissoles, pages 34-35, or with your favorite won ton or spring roll recipes. The ingredients are simple and those which you would usually keep on hand. Make this sauce at least thirty minutes ahead; the flavors keep getting better and better.

> **1 cup rice vinegar**
> **1/2 cup water**
> **1/2 cup sugar**
> **3 large garlic cloves, smashed**
> **3 tablespoons ketchup**
> **Pinch salt**
> **1 to 3 teaspoons ground fresh chili paste (sambal oelek)**

In a medium-size saucepan, combine vinegar, water and sugar. Cook over low heat 3 to 4 minutes or until sugar is dissolved. Cool and stir in remaining ingredients. Cover and refrigerate leftover sauce. Makes about 1-3/4 cups.

Spicy Soy Sauce Dip

China

This wonderful spicy dipping sauce tastes best when made thirty minutes ahead to allow the flavors time to blend. For this dip, I prefer to use less-salty medium Japanese soy sauce. Serve with deep fried and steamed snacks. Leftover sauce can be used within two days as a seasoning ingredients for soups or noodle dishes. (Photo on page 39.)

> **1/2 cup medium Japanese soy sauce**
> **1 cup water**
> **2 teaspoons sugar**
> **2 tablespoons rice vinegar**
> **1/2 teaspoon hot-pepper sauce or to taste**
> **1 green onion, finely minced**
> **1 large garlic clove, minced**
> **1 teaspoon sesame seed oil**

In a small bowl, combine all ingredients. Stir well to dissolve sugar. Serve in small individual serving dishes for dipping. Makes about 3/4 cup.

SWEET TEMPTATIONS

In most of Asia, there is no tradition of sweet foods being served at the close of a meal, yet the Asian people have a voracious sweet tooth. Meals are often ended with exquisitely carved, flavorful fresh fruits. I enjoy offering my guests slices of fresh tropical fruits with a serving of Spiced Green Tea Ice Cream, page 152, or Litchi Fruit Ice Cream, page 151. If you wish to serve something more, offer The Ultimate Chinese Almond Cookie, page 154. In China as well as in other parts of Asia, a specially prepared sweet dish might interceed the courses of a formal banquet. Follow Chinese custom and delight your guests with a tea cup of Mandarin Orange Fruit Soup, page 53, between selected courses of your next special oriental dinner. If your main course is spicy-hot, a serving of Hot Ginger Tea, page 143, between courses or at the end of the meal will serve as a soothing digestive, thanks to ginger-root's medicinal properties.

Sweet foods are considered snack foods throughout much of Asia and are usually meant to be accompanied by a cup of steaming hot tea. Because of European influences upon Indonesia and Malaysia, Western-style pastries, cakes and cookies supplement the diet as well as native sweets made with rice flour and coconut milk. Spiced Macadamia Nut Cake with Coconut-Lime Glaze, page 146, might be served as a between-meal snack or during a British-influenced afternoon tea. In the Philippine Islands, traditional sweets such as Bibinka, page 157, are served at Merienda or afternoon tea.

In Japan, the sweet tooth is often satisfied with delicious, small sponge cakes in an assortment of rainbow colors. These cakes are baked in the European tradition. But, typical of most foreign ideas which have been assimilated into Japan's culture, they end up being distinctively Japanese. Meiko's Ginger-Flavored Sweet Wine Cake, page 147, is a delicious example

Because of British influences, sweet dishes do follow an Indian meal, although fresh fruit or a refreshing dish of ice cream would be nice as well. There is no end to the number of homemade sweets for sale in Indian markets. Many, as well as ice creams and puddings, are made with reduced sweetened milk. Fragrant Rose Dumplings, page 150, is made with a quick and easy reduced milk substitute. This sweet is often served in Indian restaurants.

Autumn Moon Cakes

China

These small stuffed cakes are traditionally eaten in China in celebration of the Autumn Moon Festival celebrated in the eighth lunar month on the fifteenth day. In the fourteenth century, Chinese cooks aided their country against Mongolian conquerors by stuffing secret messages for a plan of attack inside moon cake dough. The moon cakes were widely distributed; the rebellion was a success! It was to be the beginning of the end of the powerful rule of the Northern invaders. Autumn Moon Cakes also contain surprises, but of a tastier nature. Spice-scented cookie-like dough surrounds a rich filling of dates, prunes and orange. Sometimes I hide a whole blanched almond or a quail-egg-size ball of almond paste inside the filling of each mooncake. These are substitutes for duck eggs, sometimes tucked inside large moon cakes in China.

Date & Prune Paste:
8 ounces whole pitted dates, chopped
6 ounces whole pitted prunes, chopped
Freshly grated peel 1 small orange
1 cup fresh orange juice
2 tablespoons sugar
1 tablespoon fresh lemon juice
Pinch salt
1 tablespoon butter
1/4 cup flaked coconut
1/4 cup toasted pine nuts, chopped toasted blanched almonds or chopped toasted
    walnuts
1/2 teaspoon vanilla extract

Moon Cake Dough:
2-1/2 cups sifted all-purpose flour, lightly spooned into cup
1/2 cup packed light-brown sugar
1/2 teaspoon salt
1/2 teaspoon five-spice powder
1/2 cup unsalted butter, chilled, cut in small pieces
1/2 cup vegetable shortening
1/2 teaspoon vanilla extract
1 to 2 teaspoons water, if needed

Grease 10 (3-inch) ruffled or fluted tartlet pans or brioche pans. Prepare Date & Prune Paste and Moon Cake Dough. To form moon cakes, divide Moon Cake Dough in 10 even-sized balls. Dust 1 ball in flour. Flatten in a circle about 3- to 3-1/2-inches in diameter. Place 1 tablespoon of Date & Prune Paste in center of dough. Fold dough gently around paste in a ball. Repeat with remaining dough and filling. Press balls into greased pans; press tops flat. Set pans on a baking sheet. Chill at least 1 hour or up to several hours.

Preheat oven to 325F (165C). Bake on baking sheet in preheated oven 25 to 30 minutes or until golden-brown. Cool 5 minutes. Run a small knife gently around edge of pans. Invert and remove pans. Cool completely. Slice in wedges. Store in an air-tight container up to several days. Makes 10 moon cakes.

Date & Prune Paste:
In a medium-size saucepan, combine dates, prunes, orange peel and juice, sugar, lemon juice and salt. Cook over medium-low heat about 20 minutes or until thickened. Stir often, increasing stirring as paste becomes thicker and slightly dry. If necessary, reduce heat as paste thickens to prevent burning. Stir in butter, coconut, nuts and vanilla. Use at once or refrigerate in a covered container until needed. Makes about 2-1/4 cups.

Moon Cake Dough:
In a medium-size bowl, mix flour, brown sugar, salt and five-spice powder with hands. Add butter and shortening by large spoonfuls. Sprinkle with vanilla. With hands, work fat into flour until mixture becomes crumbly and forms a ball. If mixture is dry, add enough water to work mixture until a ball is formed. Use at once or wrap and refrigerate until needed. Let dough stand at room temperature until workable. Makes about 1/2 pound dough.

Hot Ginger Tea

Throughout Asia, fresh gingerroot is valued for its medicinal and digestive qualities as well as its pungent taste. Few beverages are more soothing than a cup of aromatic hot ginger tea. The addition of toasted pine nuts is a distinctive Korean touch, a wonderful flavor and textural contrast for the silken-smooth, sweet spicy tea.

> **1 quart water**
> **1/3 pound fresh gingerroot, peeled, thinly sliced, smashed**
> **1 cup dark-brown sugar**
> **Pinch salt**
> **1/4 cup toasted pine nuts**

In a medium-size saucepan, combine water, gingerroot, brown sugar and salt. Simmer, partially covered, over medium-low heat 30 minutes. If stronger tea is desired, simmer longer. Strain and serve hot in Japanese-style teacups. Add 2 teaspoons of nuts to each cup of tea. Makes 6 Japanese-size teacup servings.

VARIATION
To prepare *Ginger Almond Tea*, add 1 tablespoon almond liqueur to 1 cup hot ginger tea.

HINT
Tea can be left at room temperature several hours, then reheated, or cooled and refrigerated overnight. Remove ginger slices before reheating.

To prepare **Taiwanese Pineapple Wedding Cake**, *press half of the Moon Cake Dough into a fluted tart pan with deep sides and a removable bottom. Spoon the tart pineapple conserve filling into the prepared dough.*

Spread Almond Icing over the warm pastry and decorate with glacé fruits and nuts to make a spectacular presentation for any special occasion.

Sweet Rice Soup with Pine Nuts   *Korea*

Hearty Korean soup, made of sweet glutinous rice with red beans, is always prepared in celebration of the first full moon of the year. This sweet version offers a sampler of the tastes and textures the Koreans love so well. Present the condiments in small dishes to be passed on the side.

      1/2 cup sweet glutinous rice
      6 cups water or as needed
      3/4 to 1 cup sugar
      1 teaspoon vanilla extract
      Dash salt
      1/2 cup toasted pine nuts or toasted walnut pieces
      1/3 cup chopped dates
      1/3 cup golden raisins
      1/2 cup pineapple chunks, cut in small pieces
      1 large apple-pear, peeled, cored, diced
      Ground cinnamon
      1/2 cup Japanese sweetened red beans (azuke)
      1/3 cup diced dried persimmons or dried apricots

Rinse rice in a medium-size bowl of cool water, removing any foreign material. Pour off milky water. Continue rinsing until water runs clear. Cover rice with fresh water; soak overnight. Drain rice. In a medium-size saucepan, simmer rice and water over medium-low heat until rice is tender. Thin with additional water if mixture thickens beyond the porridge stage. Stir in sugar, vanilla, salt and nuts. Serve soup in small bowls. Invite guests to add remaining ingredients to soup, as desired. Makes 6 to 8 servings.

Taiwanese Pineapple Wedding Cake   *Taiwan*

This spectacular-looking pastry features a tart pineapple-conserve filling and a buttery shortbread dough flavored with a hint of five-spice powder. It is similar to a special-celebration sweet made in certain regions in Taiwan. Heavy decorative shallow molds for shaping the cake are available in Taiwan. You can substitute a decorative metal tart pan, available in cookware stores. The soft pliable dough can be molded in a variety of interesting shapes and sizes.

2 recipes Moon Cake Dough, pages 142-143
Glacé pineapple
Glacé red and green cherries
1/4 cup pine nuts
Blanched whole almonds
Additional pine nuts

Pineapple Conserve:
1 (20-oz.) can crushed pineapple in natural juice
1-1/4 cups sugar
2 tablespoons fresh lemon juice
1 teaspoon freshly grated lemon peel
1/2 teaspoon five-spice powder
1 tablespoon butter
1/2 teaspoon vanilla extract

Almond Icing:
2 cups powdered sugar
2 teaspoons almond extract
1/4 cup hot water

Prepare Pineapple Conserve. Divide Moon Cake Dough in half. Press 1 piece of dough over bottom and 1 inch up sides of a 10-inch fluted tart pan with deep sides and a removable bottom. Spread Pineapple Conserve evenly over pastry. Sprinkle with 1/4 cup pine nuts. Between sheets of waxed paper, roll out remaining dough in a 10-inch circle, leaving edges slightly thinner than middle. Remove top sheet of waxed paper. Invert pastry circle over filling; pull off remaining sheet of waxed paper. Press edges of top and bottom pastry together to seal edges. Level edges and smooth top. Cover and chill at least 1 hour or overnight.

Preheat oven to 325F (165C). Remove cover from pastry. Set pan on a baking sheet. Bake in preheated oven on middle rack 30 minutes or until crisp and tan-colored. Cool 30 minutes. Invert on a large serving plate. Prepare Almond Icing; spread over top of slightly warm pastry. Cool completely until icing is set. Decorate iced pastry with glacé fruits, almonds and additional pine nuts. Cut in wedges. Makes 16 or more servings.

Pineapple Conserve:
In a medium-size saucepan, combine pineapple with juice, sugar, lemon juice and peel and five-spice powder. Cook slowly, stirring occasionally, over medium-low heat about 40 minutes or until liquid is reduced and pineapple is thick and slightly candied. Remove from heat; stir in butter and vanilla. Cool and use at once. Or cover tightly and refrigerate up to 2 weeks. Makes about 2 cups.

Almond Icing:
In a medium-size bowl, combine all ingredients until smooth. Makes about 2 cups.

Spiced Macadamia Nut Cake with Coconut-Lime Glaze

Malaysia

The Nonya women of Malaysia are imaginative and creative bakers. Many traditional Nonya cakes are based upon rice flour, coconut milk, tropical fruits, a variety of nuts and rich spices. They are wonderful gaudy colorful affairs, often tinted colors of the rainbow. European-style baking is also much admired. Nonya cooks have adapted the techniques to their native ingredients, creating a new category of East-West confections. In this spice cake, macadamia nuts are an excellent substitute for the rich-tasting Malaysian candlenuts which are difficult to find.

1 cup cake flour
1/4 teaspoon baking soda
1/4 teaspoon baking powder
1/2 teaspoon salt
1/4 teaspoon ground tumeric
1/4 teaspoon freshly ground cardamon
1/4 teaspoon freshly ground nutmeg
1/2 cup unsalted butter, room temperature
1 cup sugar
2 large eggs, separated, room temperature
1/4 cup bananna puree
1/2 teaspoon coconut extract
1/4 cup Light Coconut Milk, page 21, canned coconut milk or plain milk
1/4 cup coarsely chopped macadamia, cashew or Brazil nuts
1/16 teaspoon cream of tartar

Coconut-Lime Glaze:
1 tablespoon fresh lime juice
1 tablespoon Light Coconut Milk, page 21, canned coconut milk or plain milk
1/4 cup powdered sugar
1-1/2 teaspoons freshly grated lime peel

Preheat oven to 325F (165C). Grease a 9'' x 5'' loaf pan. In a small bowl, sift flour with baking soda, baking powder, salt and spices. In a medium-size bowl, cream butter. Reserve 1 tablespoon of sugar. Gradually beat remaining sugar into butter until creamy. Beat in egg yolks. By hand, blend in banana puree and coconut extract. Add 1/2 of flour mixture and 2 tablespoons of Light Coconut Milk; stir until flour disappears. Stir in remaining flour mixture, coconut milk and nuts. With an electric mixer, whip egg whites on low speed 1 minute; gradually increase speed to medium-high. When egg whites are foamy, sprinkle with reserved sugar and cream of tartar. Continue beating until stiff and glossy but not dry.

With a large spatula, fold 1/3 of egg whites into batter. Give bowl a quarter turn each folding motion. Fold in remaining egg whites until blended. Pour batter into greased pan. Bake about 35 minutes or until a wooden pick inserted in center comes out clean.

Prepare Coconut-Lime Glaze. With a bamboo skewer or wooden pick, poke small holes over top of cake. Pour on glaze while hot. Cool completely before slicing. Makes 8 to 10 servings.

Lime Glaze:
In a small bowl, combine all ingredients. Makes about 1/4 cup.

Meiko's Ginger-Flavored Sweet Wine Cake

Japan

Throughout Japan you can buy a popular golden spongecake called "kat-su-tera." Introduced by the Portuguese as "castilla" to 18th century Japan, the cake was adopted and modified to suit Japanese taste. Usually purchased in bakeries and department stores, the cake is available in a variety of interesting shapes and flavors. Japanese housewives with home ovens enjoy baking their special versions. This recipe is a treasure, generously shared by Meiko Yamazaki of Yokohama, Japan. I have transcribed her recipe, cutting it in half. It is moist and tender without the addition of fat. The high sugar content encourages moistness, but Meiko mellows flavor and texture further by adding Japanese sweet rice wine. Seek out the best rice wine you can find, that which is naturally brewed, aged and sweetened with no added preservatives. Meiko recommends baking the cake two to three days in advance of serving. Although delicious plain, I often use it as the base for other desserts or lavish it with fresh fruit and whipped cream.

> **1 cup sugar**
> **1/4 cup honey**
> **3 tablespoons Japanese sweet rice wine (mirin)**
> **1 tablespoon fresh ginger juice**
> **1 tablespoon fresh lemon juice**
> **1/4 teaspoon salt**
> **6 jumbo eggs or 7 large eggs, separated**
> **1 cup sifted cake flour**
> **1/8 teaspoon cream of tartar**

Preheat oven to 325F (165C). Line a 10-inch-square deep-sided pan with parchment or waxed paper. Lightly grease bottom of paper; do not grease sides. Reserve 1 tablespoon of sugar. In a medium-size bowl, whisk remaining sugar, honey, wine, ginger and lemon juice and salt into egg yolks. Place bowl in a large pan of hot water. Stir constantly 1 minute or until warm. With an electric mixer, beat 8 to 10 minutes on medium-high speed until tripled in size. Gently fold in sifted flour.

Wash beaters carefully to remove all traces of egg yolk. In a large greasefree bowl, beat egg whites with an electric mixer on low speed 1 minute; gradually increase speed to medium-high. When egg whites are foamy, sprinkle in reserved sugar and cream of tartar. Continue beating until stiff and glossy but not dry.

With a large spatula, spoon 1/3 of egg whites on top of egg batter. Cut down into middle of mixture. Bring spatula up along side of bowl, folding batter over. Give bowl a quarter turn. Fold in 1/2 of remaining egg whites. Fold in remaining egg whites in same way just until blended. Pour batter into prepared pan. Tap lightly on counter 1 to 2 times.

Bake in preheated oven on middle rack 25 minutes or until golden-brown. Cake sides will pull away slightly and top will feel spongy when pressed with finger. Cool 20 minutes. Run a small knife between edge of cake and pan. Invert on a slightly damp kitchen towel and remove pan. Pull off paper; cool completely. Cut in small square or rectangular pieces. Or wrap cake airtight and store at room temperature or refrigerate. Cake is delicious served at once yet improves with age. Makes 10 to 12 servings.

VARIATION
Substitute 1 teaspoon freshly grated lemon or orange peel or freshly grated ground nutmeg for ginger juice.

Teahouse Golden Custard Tartlets   *South China*

This is my favorite sweet pastry from the wide selection offered during a Contonese tea lunch. Inevitably, I always fly out of Hong Kong clutching a bagful, perhaps as a small consolation for having to leave. These taste best served warm from the oven. To serve warm from the oven for a special occasion, prepare the Custard Filling and line the pans with the pastry hours in advance. At the last minute, fill the chilled pastry shells, then pop them into the oven to bake.

1 recipe Golden Flaky Pastry, page 28, well chilled

Custard Filling:
1 large egg
3 large egg yolks
1/2 cup sugar
1/2 cup half and half
1/4 cup whipping cream
1 teaspoon vanilla extract
Pinch salt
1/8 teaspoon nutmeg

Prepare Custard Filling. Preheat oven to 400F (205C). On a lightly floured surface, roll out chilled Golden Flaky Pastry to an approximate 15-inch square about 1/8-inch thick. Cut out 12 to 13 pastry circles with a metal 4-inch fluted-edged or plain-edged cutter. Make a clean sharp cut so pastry edges are not mashed, preventing layer formation. Layer scraps and chill. Gently press circles into 3-inch tartlet pans or a muffin tin. Place filled pans on a baking sheet. Spoon about 3 tablespoons of filling into each pastry shell.

Bake on baking sheet in preheated oven on middle rack 10 minutes. Reduce heat to 350F (175C). Bake 3 to 5 minutes more or until pastry is crisp and separates in layers. Filling will set and become slightly puffy. Watch carefully to prevent burning. Cool 5 minutes. Filling will settle upon cooling. Run a small knife between outside edge of pastry shells and pans. Carefully remove tartlets. Serve at once or within several hours. Cover and refrigerate leftovers. Serve leftover tartlets cold or at room temperature. Makes 12 to 13 tartlets.

Custard Filling:
In a medium-size bowl, whisk egg, egg yolks, sugar, half and half and whipping cream. Stir in vanilla, salt and nutmeg. Spoon off any foam on top of filling. Let stand 1 hour at room temperature. Makes about 1-1/2 cups.

VARIATION
To prepare *Teahouse Golden Custard Tartlets with Coconut*, substitute 1 teaspoon coconut extract for vanilla extract. Sprinkle 1 teaspoon shredded sweetened coconut on each tartlet before baking.

Top right: Rose Dumplings, page 150; Right to left on lower plate: The Ultimate Chinese Almond Cookie, page 154; Teahouse Golden Custard Tartlets; Pastry Pumpkins with Spiced Green Tea Ice Cream, page 153

Rose Dumplings

India

In India this popular sweet is made from a thick, dough-like boiled-milk product. You can prepare an excellent substitute for this thick milk cheese by mixing nonfat dry milk with cream cheese. Rose water is used in India to flavor sweets, rice and meat dishes and beverages. It is added to sweetened rich yogurt to make "lassi," a delicious and nutritious drink. Use rose water to perfume the syrup for soaking "gulub jaman" (Rose Dumplings). Purchase rose water at specialty food shops, Asian markets or Middle Eastern stores. Rose Syrup can be used as a table syrup for flavoring hot coffee or tea, spooned over puddings and ice cream or mixed with sparkling water and rose petals to make a refreshing summertime cooler. (Photo on page 149.)

1/2 cup nonfat dry milk powder
1/2 (3-oz.) package cream cheese, room temperature
1/2 teaspoon almond extract
1 tablespoon butter, melted
2 tablespoons flour
1/4 teaspoon baking powder
1 heaping tablespoon vanilla-flavored or plain yogurt or as needed
4 cups peanut or vegetable oil for deep-frying
1 tablespoon chopped pistachio nuts
Rose petals, if desired

Rose Syrup:
1 cup water
1 cup sugar
1 tablespoon rose water

Prepare Rose Syrup. In a small bowl, combine dry milk powder, cream cheese, almond extract and butter. Stir in flour and baking powder. Combine until mixture is consistency of fine crumbs. Blend in yogurt to form a dough. Shape in 12 small smooth oval or round balls.

In a wok or heavy shallow saucepan, heat oil to 345 F (165 C) or until a 1-inch cube of bread turns golden-brown in 60 seconds. Fry 4 or 5 dumplings at a time, turning often, 3 to 4 minutes or until light golden-brown. Do not fry quickly or they will become tough. Drain on paper towels. Immediately place hot dumplings into warm Rose Syrup. Let stand at room temperature 1 hour or until dumplings swell from absorbing some of syrup. Sprinkle individual servings with pistachio nuts and garnish with rose petals, if desired. Serve at once. Makes 4 servings.

Rose Syrup:
In a medium-size saucepan, combine water and sugar. Bring to a boil over medium heat; cook 10 minutes. Stir in rose water. Reduce heat to lowest setting and keep syrup warm. Makes about 1-1/3 cups.

HINT
Dumplings can be covered and refrigerated up to 3 days. Serve at room temperature.

Litchi Fruit Ice Cream

Southeast Asian

Litchi fruits, sometimes called litchi nuts, have a red shell-like outer covering resembling a round strawberry. Indigenous to China, these delicious fruits are readily available in canned form in most markets. It is found fresh in some markets in July and in dried form in many Asian markets year-round, sold as a chewy snack. If you like litchi fruits, you will love this creamy litchi-flavored ice cream.

1 (20-oz.) can litchi fruits in syrup
2 large eggs
2 large egg yolks
1-1/8 cups sugar
1 cup half and half
2-1/2 cups whipping cream
1 teaspoon freshly grated lemon peel
1 tablespoon lemon juice
2 tablespoons unsalted butter
1/3 cup finely chopped macadamia nuts or blanched almonds
Pinch salt

Drain litchi fruits; reserve 1 cup of syrup. In a blender or food processor fitted with the steel blade, puree litchi fruits. Beat eggs and egg yolks in top of a double boiler. Whisk in sugar and half and half. Place over simmering water; do not allow water to touch bottom of container holding egg mixture. Cook, stirring constantly, until mixture thickens slightly and coats a spoon. Pour into a large bowl. When cool, add reserved litchi syrup, whipping cream and lemon peel and juice; stir well. Refrigerate until chilled. In a small skillet, melt butter over low heat. Sauté nuts until golden-brown. Add salt. Cool nuts; stir into chilled ice cream base. Freeze in an ice cream machine according to manufacturer's directions. Serve immediately or freeze. Makes about 2 quarts.

VARIATIONS

To prepare *Coconut Ice Cream*, omit litchi fruits and litchi syrup. Substitute 2 recipes Dairy Coconut Cream, page 20, for whipping cream. Add 1 teaspoon coconut extract.

To prepare *Rose Ice Cream*, omit litchi fruits and litchi syrup. Add 1/4 cup rose water or to taste and a few drops red food coloring. Increase whipping cream to 3-1/2 cups.

Noodles are always served at birthday parties or other special occasions with the hope they will bring long life and good luck to the birthday recipient and the guests. Whichever noodle dish you might decide to serve, heed a word of warning! Please remember NOT to cut the noodles; slurping is allowed. You might reverse everyone's good fortune and create havoc instead!

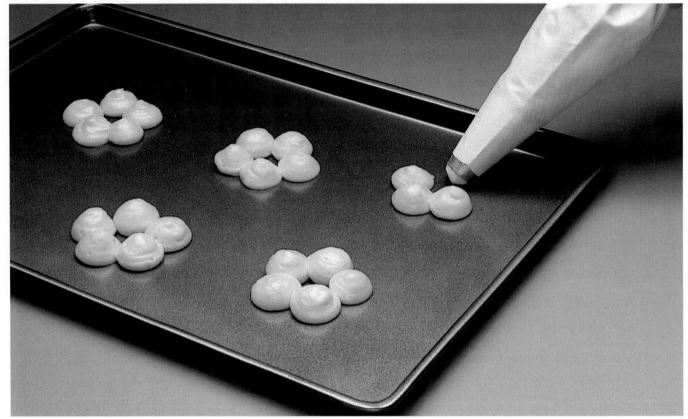

To prepare **Pastry Pumpkins with Spiced Green Tea Ice Cream**, *spoon the Golden Egg Puff Paste into a pastry bag fitted with a half-inch nozzle. Pipe the paste in five mounds to form a circle.*

Spiced Green Tea Ice Cream   *Japan*

Green tea ice cream is often made with "matcha," an expensive special powdered green tea used for the formal tea ceremony in Japan. "Gyokuro" (jewel dew), the leaf form of "matcha," or "sencha," an excellent quality tea, can be substituted. Use the best loose-leaf green tea you can find.

> **1 cup half and half**
> **1 tablespoon top-quality loose-leaf green tea**
> **1/2 cup sugar**
> **1/4 cup orange blossom honey**
> **1 pint whipping cream**
> **1/8 teaspoon salt**
> **1 teaspoon freshly grated lemon peel**
> **1 teaspon fresh lemon juice**
> **1/2 teaspoon vanilla extract**
> **1/4 teaspoon ground nutmeg**
> **1/2 teaspoon ground ginger**
> **Small amount moss-green paste food coloring or 3 drops liquid food coloring**

In a small saucepan, heat half and half over low heat until hot. Add tea; remove from heat. Steep 5 minutes. Strain through a fine strainer into a large bowl. Discard tea leaves. Stir sugar and honey into hot mixture until dissolved; cool to room temperature. Stir in remaining ingredients. Chill ice cream base; freeze in an ice cream machine according to manufacturer's directions. Serve at once or freeze. Makes 6 servings.

Pastry Pumpkins with
Spiced Green Tea Ice Cream   *Japan*

There's a frost in the pumpkin patch! These adorable chilled pastry pumpkins are filled with delectable green tea ice cream, but any of your favorite flavors would be just as good. They make wonderful appetizers or snacks filled with Macadamia Chicken Spread, Princess Hats, page 40, or Spicy Pork with Bamboo Shoots, Spicy Pork with Bamboo Shoots in Pastry Baskets, pages 84-85. Substitute green pepper stems for candy stems. (Photo on page 149.)

1 recipe Golden Egg Puff Paste, page 29
Few drops red food coloring, if desired
1 recipe Spiced Green Tea Ice Cream, opposite page, prepared at least 24 hours
  in advance
Candied green pineapple or flattened green gum drops, cut in small
  stem-shaped pieces
Powdered sugar, if desired

Preheat oven to 400F (205C). Lightly grease and flour a baking sheet. Tint Golden Egg Puff Paste with food coloring, if desired. Spoon Golden Egg Puff Paste into a pastry bag fitted with a 1/2-inch nozzle. To form each pastry pumpkin, pipe 5 mounds of paste about 1-inch in diameter in a circle with sides barely touching. There will be a small opening in center. If necessary, smooth tops lightly with a small brush dipped in water.

Bake in preheated oven 15 to 18 minutes or until deep golden-orange and hollow and dry inside. Puffs will expand to rounded pumpkin shapes. Cool completely on a wire rack. Using a serrated knife, carefully cut off top 1/3 of each pumpkin. Fill each pumpkin with a small scoop of Spiced Green Tea Ice Cream. Replace top. Push a "stem" of candied green pineapple into top of each pumpkin. Dust a small amount of powdered sugar "snow" on top, if desired. Makes 6 servings.

HINT
Filled pastry pumpkins can be frozen in a single layer in an airtight freezer container up to 1 week.

The Ultimate Chinese Almond Cookie   *China*

These Chinese almond cookies are a triple almond delight! Almond extract, chopped almonds and almond paste add a new dimension to the traditional Chinese version. You will love the shortbread texture and intense almond taste. Long slow baking is crucial; the cookies must be dried to delicate crispness without excessive browning. Lard is traditionally used to create melt-in-the-mouth texture and distinctive taste. If possible, avoid processed lard. Use rendered fresh leaf lard which is the fat that lines the abdominal wall of a pig. If you are an almond lover, you will agree these heavenly cookies are worthy of the gods! I am sure my offering has pleased Tsao Chun, the powerful Chinese kitchen God, patron of cooks and controller of fate in kitchen. His silent image holds court from my kitchen wall keeping mental score of my culinary triumphs and disasters. (Photo on page 149.)

1 cup top-quality leaf lard, divided in 4 pieces
1 (7-oz.) roll almond paste, cut in 6 to 8 pieces
1 cup sugar
3 large eggs
1-1/2 tablespoons almond extract
1/2 teaspoon baking soda
8 to 10 drops yellow food coloring, if desired
1/3 cup finely chopped toasted blanched almonds
3-1/2 cups sifted soft-wheat flour, spooned lightly into cup
Additional sugar
18 blanched whole almonds

In a large bowl, beat lard and almond paste until soft and creamy with an electric mixer. Add sugar; continue beating until smooth. Add 2 eggs, beating well after each addition. Beat in almond extract, baking soda and food coloring, if desired. Stop mixer. Add chopped almonds. Sprinkle in 1 cup of flour. Mix at lowest speed until flour begins to disappear. Add remaining flour by cupful. When ingredients are blended, cover dough and refrigerate overnight.

Preheat oven to 250F (120C). Line baking sheets with parchment or waxed paper. Divide dough in 16 to 18 (1/4-cup) pieces. Roll each piece in a ball. Place balls on prepared baking sheets, allowing at least 1 inch between each ball for expansion. Oil bottom of a 1-cup dry measure or flat-bottom glass; press on a plate of additonal sugar. Using bottom of sugared cup as a cookie press, flatten each ball to a 3-inch circle. To prevent sticking, coat bottom of cup with sugar each time before pressing. In a small bowl, beat remaining egg. Brush surface of each cookie with beaten egg. Press a whole almond into center of each cookie.

Bake in preheated oven 45 minutes or until crispy and dry. If cookies brown too quickly, reduce heat to 225F (105C). Cookies can baked in oven with heat reduced to 200F (95C) 1-1/2 to 2 hours or until crispy and dry. Remove cookies from baking sheets; cool completely. Cookies become slightly crisper when cool. Store up to 4 weeks in an airtight container. Flavor improves with age. Makes 16 to 18 cookies.

VARIATION
For a more intense almond flavor, substitute 1 (7-oz.) roll amaretti paste for almond paste.

Indonesian-Style Pineapple Dessert Centerpiece, pages 156-157

Indonesian-Style Pineapple Dessert Centerpiece

Indonesia

Fabulous fresh fruit is a refreshing end for any oriental meal. But do it with style; delight your guests with a platter of beautifully arranged fruits surrounding a hollowed pineapple boat filled with tangy Pineapple-Coconut Cream. (Photo on page 155.)

1 large fresh pineapple, heavy and fragrant with fresh-looking fronds
Ti or banana leaves or leaf lettuce
2 kiwifruits, peeled, sliced, slices cut in half
3 tablespoons coarsely chopped macadamia nuts
Fresh unsprayed edible flowers, if desired

Pineapple-Coconut Cream:
1 (8-1/2-oz.) can crushed pineapple packed in natural juice
1 large egg, slightly beaten
1/3 cup sugar
1 heaping teaspoon all-purpose flour
3 tablespoons fresh lemon juice
1/8 teaspoon salt
2 to 3 drops yellow food coloring, if desired
1 tablespoon unsalted butter
1 teaspoon vanilla extract
1 cup Dairy Coconut Cream, page 20, or plain whipping cream, well chilled

Fruit Platter:
Pineapple pieces from pineapple boat
1 to 2 baskets fresh strawberries
1 (10-oz.) can litchi fruits, drained, stuffed with whole macadamia nuts
2 navel oranges, peeled, sliced
2 ripe mangos, peeled, sliced
1 fragrant ripe honeydew melon, peeled, seeded, cubed
1 fragrant ripe cantaloupe, peeled, seeded, cubed
4 to 5 star fruits (carambola), sliced
2 apple-pears, peeled, sliced
1/4 pound fresh red cherries with stems
6 small kumquats
Small bunch champagne grapes
Pomegranate seeds, if desired
Thin shreds orange peel, if desired

Prepare Pineapple-Coconut Cream. Slice off top 1/3 of pineapple lengthwise. With a small knife, cut into large portion of pineapple. Remove fruit and reserve. Do not cut through bottom; preserve boat shape of pineapple. Drain shell; blot juices with paper towels. Refrigerate in an airtight plastic bag until needed.

Line a large platter with ti leaves. Spoon Pineapple-Coconut Cream into pineapple shell. Place kiwifruit slices, rounded sides up, into filling around edge of pineapple shell. Sprinkle cream filling with nuts. Arrange Fruit Platter selections in an attractive design around pineapple shell. Sprinkle litchi fruits with pomegranate seeds, if desired. Sprinkle honeydew melon with orange peel, if desired. Decorate with fresh flowers, if desired. Makes 6 servings.

Pineapple-Coconut Cream:

In a medium-size saucepan, combine pineapple with juice, egg, sugar, flour, lemon juice, salt and food coloring, if desired. Blend well. Cook, stirring constantly, over medium heat until mixture thickens. Remove from heat; stir in butter and vanilla. Cool completely. Cover and refrigerate until chilled or overnight. In a small chilled bowl, whip Dairy Coconut Cream to soft peaks. Fold into chilled pineapple mixture. Use at once or refrigerate up to 2 hours. Makes about 3-1/2 cups.

Fruit Platter:

Cut reserved pineapple in cubes. Select 6 to 7 fruits. Fruits can be prepared 2 to 3 hours ahead, covered and refrigerated until needed.

Bibinka   *Philippine Islands*

Bibinka is a sweet coconut rice cake from the Philippines. This Bibinka recipe is similar to "mochi," the Japanese chewy, pounded-rice snack sometimes made with "mochiko," which is finely ground, uncooked glutinous rice flour. But Bibinka is more cake-like, richer-tasting and absolutely delicious. Sometimes cheese made from caribou or water buffalo's milk or even Parmesan or mild Cheddar cheese is added to Bibinka. I like to vary the ingredients, often adding golden raisins or chopped nuts. This recipe was featured at an international food festival sponsored by my son's school in Japan. It came from the convent kitchen belonging to the order of Filipino nuns charged with running the school.

> **2-1/2 cups glutinous rice flour (mochiko)**
> **1-1/2 cups packed light-brown sugar**
> **1 cup granulated sugar**
> **1/4 teaspoon salt**
> **1 tablespoon baking powder**
> **2 large eggs**
> **1/4 cup butter, melted**
> **2 cups Rich Coconut Milk, page 21, or canned coconut milk**
> **1 teaspoon coconut extract**
> **1 cup sweetened shredded coconut**
> **1/3 cup finely chopped walnuts, blanched almonds, peanuts or macadamia nuts,**
>   **if desired**

Preheat oven to 350F (175C). Lightly grease a 13'' x 9'' baking pan. In a blender or food processor fitted with the steel blade, process flour, 1 cup of brown sugar, granulated sugar, salt and baking powder a few seconds to mix ingredients. Add eggs, butter, Rich Coconut Milk and coconut extract. Blend until smooth. Pour batter into greased pan. In a medium-size bowl, combine remaining brown sugar, coconut and nuts, if desired. Sprinkle evenly over top of cake. Bake in preheated oven 45 minutes or until cake is set and topping is golden-brown. Cool and cut in small squares and eat as finger snacks. Store up to 2 days in an air-tight container. Makes 10 to 12 servings.

VARIATION
Stir 1 (8-oz.) package cream cheese, diced, or 1 cup shredded mild Cheddar cheese into batter before baking.

MAIL ORDER LIST

Dean & DeLuca
110 Green Street
Suite 304
New York, NY 10012
(800) 221-7714
 Basmati rice, food products.

Hobson Gardens
Route 2 Box 154 C
Roswell, NM 88201
(505) 622-7289
 Full line of red and green chili products.

Maid of Scandinavia
3244 Raleigh Avenue
Minneapolis, MN 55416
 Write for a catalog: baking and cooking equipment, food ingredients for baking.

Matagiri
224 East 59th Street
New York, NY 10022
(212) 755-3566
 Oriental food products, cooking equipment.

McCormick & Co., Inc.
115 Brand Road
Salem, VA 24156
 Spice and gift catalog, $2.00.

Plants of the Southwest
1812 Second Street
Santa Fe, NM 87501
(505) 983-1548
 100 page catalog; chili seeds, heirloom vegetable seeds, much more, $1.00.

Rafu Bussan Inc.
326 East 2nd Street
Los Angeles, CA 90012
 Japanese food products, cooking equipment.

Roswell Seed Company
115-117 South Main
P.O. Box 725
Roswell, MN 88201
(505) 622-7011
 Catalog available. Wholesale and retail chili seeds as well as a variety of other types of seeds for edible gardening.

Seeds Blum
Idaho City Stage
Boise, ID 83706
 Many varieties of hot chili seeds, eighteen varieties of exotic eggplant seeds. Catalog $2.00, contains information on gourmet specialties and edible gardening hints.

Spice and Sweet Mahal
135 Lexington Avenue
New York, NY 10016
(212) 683-0900
 Basmati rice, Indian spices and foods.

Texmati
Texas Rice Production Company
P.O. Box 1305
Alvan, TX 77512
(713) 331-8245
 Texmati rice.

The Pepper Gal
Dorothy L. Van Vleck
10536 119th Avenue North
Largo, FL 33543
 Over 200 varieties of chili seeds. Send self-addressed stamped envelope with inquiries.

Uwajimaya
P.O. Box 3003
Seattle, WA 98114
(206) 624-6248
 Oriental food products, cooking equipment.

White Lily Flour Company
P.O. Box 871
Knoxville, TN 37901
(615) 546-5511
 Soft-wheat southern flour.

INDEX